Connecting the Dots

A Layman's Application of Sumerian Archeology to Biblical Text

J. Dukas Ringelheim

Copyright © 2023 by J. Dukas Ringelheim
Typesetting and Cover by Jeanette Goldstein

First Edition, 2023

All rights reserved. No part of this book may be reproduced in any form or by any electronic or mechanical means, including information storage and retrieval systems, without permission in writing from the author, except by a reviewer who may quote brief passages in a review.

9798870152103, hardcover

juliusringelheim@gmail.com

Contents

Forward 5

Introduction 7

Chapter One: The Importance of Rereading the Bible Using the Lens of Archeology 11

Chapter Two: Abraham and Sodom (*Genesis* 14) 15

Chapter Three: The Seeming Israelite Obsession with Meat 27

Chapter Four: Abraham–Moses Connection 35

Chapter Five: Brit Bain Habasorim (BBH)–Brit Milah (*Genesis*:15,16,17) 41

Chapter Six: Brit Bain Habasorim–Brit Milah, Binding of Isaak 53

Chapter Seven: Sarah, the Mother of the Jewish People 63

Chapter Eight: Suzerain-Vassal Treaty 75

Chapter Nine: Wells: Welcome to Canaan 81

Chapter Ten: Hagar & Ishmael (Competition Challenges Everyone) 89

Chapter Eleven: *Leviticus* 23:23-25 Explained 101

Chapter Twelve: Jewish Holidays: Some Unexpected Insights from Sumeria 105

Endnotes   121

Forward

I never intended to write another book, let alone a sequel to *The Genius of Abraham*. However, after a few revitalizing breaths, it became apparent to me that I had left many insights unshared. I want to give a special thanks to my friends — Ira Berman, Menachem Mendlowitz, Aaron Steinfeld, and Rochelle Turetsky — for patiently listening to and commenting on these thoughts before I wrote them down.

The analysis provided in these pages is based on the level of insight called *peshat*. It is not rooted in Rabbinical interpretation or mystical Kabbalah. Instead, we rely on reading the text, translating it, and then interpreting it based on three rules.

1. Where else in the Torah are there similar words or symbolism?

2. What information about ancient Sumerian, Egyptian, or Mesopotamian culture can help to explain the text?

3. How does the text support the tenets of monotheism?

When evaluated against these rules, new and insightful understandings of the text quickly come to light. Every effort to reach new understandings is expressed with respect to and dove-tailed with existing Rabbinical commentaries.

Introduction

For those who are discovering my project for the first time, let me take a moment to explain my methodology. When I find out about an archaeological fact regarding ancient Sumer, I look into my Bible to see if this new tidbit might allow me to better understand any unexplained or unintentionally wrongly explained passage.

Not all archaeological facts are relics. Many facts are deciphered in cuneiform manuscripts. These invaluable texts give us a glimpse into the cultural milieu that existed during the Patriarchs' time. Knowing the beliefs and practices of the era allows us to better understand the Biblical narrative. It will also give us an insight into how Abraham, as a Sumerian, saw the world. An example of Abraham seeing the world through Sumerian eyes would be his accepting Hagar, his wife's handmaiden, as a wife. From the archaeological record and confirmed in the Biblical narrative, we are informed that this was a conventional method of responding to an infertile wife (*Behind the Scenes of the Old Testament*/ Greer, Hilber & Walton, p. 191).

Biblical historians have sought to pinpoint exactly when Abraham lived. They do this by showing that Abraham's behavior reflected the social norms of the Sumer culture at a specific time in its history. This allows us to confirm when and where Abraham lived.

Another important reason for knowing the culture of Abraham's world is to get a better understanding of how he approached his world to achieve his mission. It took a deep understanding of Sumerian royalty and pagan temples to convert his Sumerian world to monotheism. We can understand the tactics he employed from the interpretation of crucial Biblical text (see *The Genius of Abraham*, pp. 10-15). Canaan presented Abraham with different challenges, revealing the meaning behind Biblical stories. A good example of this is when Abraham arrives in Canaan, he quickly understands the social hierarchy among the Canaanites. This leads him to develop a two-track effort to convert ancient Canaan (see chapter 7). This will become clearer as we move forward.

The format of this book is to list a topic, provide relevant Scriptural text, and then ask three seemingly obvious questions of the Biblical narrative. Lastly, I then supply an answer based on archaeological discoveries, always respecting the Judeo-Orthodox tradition that the Bible was given to Moses on Mount Horeb.

Following the Facts:

From the findings of modern archeology, we have become aware of the Sumerian world that Abraham was born into and eventually grew to despise. In my previous book, *The Genius of Abraham*, I could discern that the creation stories and many laws are part of an Abrahamic tradition that was then incorporated into Torahs Moshe. This novel approach resolves many questions in the text. By contrasting and comparing the Bible to Sumerian beliefs and practices we can easily detect the genius of Abraham. He instituted norms and practices that would ween the commoners away from the corrupt temples. Archeology has also uncovered, the Canaanite pagan beliefs, social hierarchies, and legal practices. When Abraham moved away from Haran, he moved from the Sumerian culture to a Semitic, Canaanite culture. These two cultures differed significantly. Sumeria was an urban, sophisticated society with a defined hierarchical structure. Canaan, by contrast, was rural and undeveloped. It had an endemic pagan belief system that was rooted in superstition and fear of natural phenomena. Abraham surely modified his methods to reflect this change in the milieu. He would need to employ new ideas to accomplish his mission of bringing the world to monotheism. By following the evidence, we will uncover Abraham's out-of-the-box thinking and uncover some remarkable truths.

One rule we adopt when doing Biblical analysis is that the Bible is neither a history book nor a science book. Everything recorded in the Bible is to promote monotheism and stand in opposition to polytheism. This reflects Abraham's mission.

We can now understand that the Bible is recording select tales from Abraham's life that highlight the new strategies he employed in Canaan to promote monotheism.

As stated above, the reader of the Biblical narrative must keep in mind that the salient characteristic shared by all the Abraham stories, other than the covenants, is that they are handed down to us as examples of Abraham's efforts to introduce monotheism first to Sumer and then Canaan. Below is a listing of the chapters where we can find an important episode in Abraham's life.

1. The seven inducements given to Abraham to go from Haran to Canaan (*Genesis* 12)
2. The visit to Egypt (ibid.)
3. Victory over the four kings who captured Sodom (*Genesis* 14). See Chapter 2 within this book.
4. Brit Bain Habasorim (*Genesis* 15). See Chapter 3 within this book.
5. Birth of Ishmael (*Genesis* 16)
6. Bris Milah (*Genesis* 17)
7. The Visitors at Mamre (*Genesis* 18)
8. The visit to Gerar (*Genesis* 20). See Chapter 4 within this book
9. Rejection of Hagar and Ishmael (*Genesis* 21)
10. The treaty with Abimelach at beer-sheva (ibid.)
11. The Binding of Issak and the final blessings to Abraham (*Genesis* 22)
12. The burial of Sarah and finding a suitable bride for Isaak

Let us highlight the episodes of Abraham's life that emphasize his efforts to bring monotheism to Canaan. From the above list of recorded events, we can segment them into two groupings: Those where Abraham is responding to heavenly directives and those where Abraham is pursuing his mission to convert Canaan. Focusing on the latter, we find four examples. They are the two visits of Abraham and Sarah to royal courts. The first visit was to Egypt and the other visit was to Gerar; the third tale is the military victory over the four Kings who had taken captive the residents of Sodom along with Lot: and lastly the treaty with Abimelach at Beer Sheva. Analyzing these four episodes in light of Sumerian archeology will show that the simple reading of these stories misses many important nuances.

In Chapter 7, (part 1) we explore the visits to the royal courts of Egypt and Gerar. We now know these are both examples of Abraham's efforts to convert the Canaanites to monotheism. It is not obvious from the text but with a little analysis, we can discern Abraham's efforts as enshrined in these iconic stories. With the information supplied by archeology, basic analysis will reveal a different perspective to what you might have been taught in Elementary School.

In Chapter 2, we do an exhaustive study of the long shadow Sodom casts on the Book of *Genesis* and we will show how Sodom's doom extends into the Book of *Numbers*. Chapter 4 explains how the Abimelach story, with its multiple facets, profoundly affected Abraham and even the Israelites during their time in Egypt.

The bulk of the other remaining stories are elements of the Suzerain-Vassal Treaty, this includes the Bris Bain Habasorim, Brit Milah, and the Binding of Isaak. These important events stand apart from the other stories and involve the legal transference of the land of Canaan to Abraham and his children. All this will be developed in chapter 5.

Chapter One:

The Importance of Rereading the Bible Using the Lens of Archeology

We are fortunate to live when information that has been hidden for four thousand years has been revealed. They have unearthed this revelation via the incredible archaeological finds of the last one hundred and fifty years and is pertinent to every student of the Bible and to anyone who has a Bible-inspired lifestyle. We can now gain insight into the culture and society that Abraham was attempting to change and the challenges he faced. Much of *Genesis* is built on Abraham's mission and the award to him and his children of the land of Canaan. The Bible shared with us many stories that relate to Abraham and his family. Biblical commentators have long held that these stories are told to us for reasons that extend beyond simple storytelling. Respecting that tradition, I hope to present information uncovered by archaeology. These archaeological finds illuminate what may have initially been understood as being only minor details in the Biblical narrative but are crucial to hidden insights. Also, through the archaeological finds, we can reveal the possible intention of the Biblical narrative. This revised narrative can be dramatically different from the currently accepted reading.

As an example of the above, We can apply modern archeology to fully understand the Biblical narrative that refers to the patriarchs and matriarchs. All three generations required that prayers/pleadings be made for a barren matriarch to produce an heir. Abraham & Sarah (*Genesis* 15:3), Isaak and Rebecca (ibid. 25:21), and Jacob and Rachel (ibid. 30:22). An uninformed student might consider that our forefathers had an uncanny knack for selecting barren women as their spouses.

Many Rabbinic commentators have claimed that these episodes are intended to emphasize the value of prayers. However, from the archaeological record, we can discern a very different importance to these episodes. Based on the unearthing of Ugaric texts that were uncovered in 1936, we get two important legends that were popular in the time of Abraham. Their names are The Legend of Aqhat and the Kirta Epics. In both stories, the heads of a kingdom are required to pray for an heir. Thus, we can now better understand why in every generation of Patriarchs and Matriarchs they were required to pray that their wombs be opened by divine intervention. It was a sign of distinction to pray to a deity and then have a positive result. Furthermore, it proved that the supplicant is worthy of divine intervention as the supplicant's prayers are heard and responded to by divine intervention.

Putting the biblical narrative in context does not contradict the Biblical commentators; it enhances their position that the birth of our patriarchs was not the result of simple biology, but they were born via divine intervention. A similar construct was found in the Canaanite tradition that expected the birth of royal heirs to be the product of prayers pled, received, and answered. This extra effort that our Matriarchs required to produce an heir was a mark of nobility. Receiving a divine response was something reserved for personal prayers from the royals and the priestly class. When the Patriarchs and Matriarchs prayed and then received a child, it proved their worthiness in the eyes of the Canaanites. Having a child effortlessly would have been considered common and could have diminished the high regard and esteem the patriarchs held in ancient Canaan. An example of the esteem Abraham had with the Canaanites is when Abraham sought to buy a burial place in Hebron.

The residents said," Listen to us, Sir. You are a prince of G-d in our midst. Take our best burial site to bury your dead...." (ibid. 23:6)

The above is an example of why knowing the archaeological finds of Sumer, Mesopotamia, and Canaan is imperative to fully understand the Biblical narrative. This book intends to support this thesis in the chapters to follow.

Chapter Two:

Abraham and Sodom (*Genesis* 14)

Biblical Backstory

Abraham has a nephew, Lot, who, in the previous chapter, joined Abraham when he left Haran. After both he and his uncle amass great wealth in Egypt, a series of disagreements break out between their herdsmen. Lot leaves Abraham to reside in Sodom. After arriving in Sodom, Lot and the entire Sodom population are captured as booty and are led into captivity. Abraham organizes and implements a successful night raid that results in the defeat of the captors and the eventual return of the Sodomites to Sodom. Before he returns the Sodomites to their land, there is a cameo appearance by the high priest at Salem. Salem is where Abraham tithes the booty, he had captured to Malchizedek, a "priest of the most high," before he returns the people to their land. Jumping to Chapter 19, where the Lord chooses to wipe out the Sodomites since they had degenerated beyond redemption. Abraham is informed of Sodom's imminent destruction by angels (ibid., 18:20). Abraham bargains a deal with the angels. The Sodomites would be spared annihilation if there were still ten morally ethical individuals in Sodom. When 10 morally un-corrupted people could not be found, the fate of the Sodomites is sealed. Angels save Lot and his family from the depraved Sodomites and the city's impending destruction.

Questions

When the Lord shares with Abraham Sodom's fate, the text writes," G-d said, "Shall I hide from Abraham what I am going to do?"(Genesis 18:17).

1. Why was Sodom entitled to special treatment by having its fate shared with Abraham?

2. The Bible says that when Abraham meets Malchizedek, he tithes the booty he collected when recapturing the Sodomites from the four kings. His interaction with this high priest of Salem is puzzling. Abraham, when referring to G-d, adopts Malchizedek's term (ibid.14:22), "E-l Elyon, the most high." El was the chief of the gods in the Canaanite pantheon and Malchizedek uses the term E-l Elyon when he greets Abraham (ibid.14:19). Abraham consistently refers to G-d as E-l Shakai

(*Genesis* 17:1) (meaning "he who is sufficient"). The Rambam in the Moreh Navuchem LXIII explains this unique term which signifies that the Creator does not require any other being for effecting the existence of what He created or the conservation of what He created. Abraham could have continued using his unique term for G-d instead he seems to adopt the Canaanite term for God in the temple of Malchizedek. What would cause Abraham to suddenly adopt this foreign name for G-d?

3. Immediately after the Bible relates the story of Abraham's success in releasing the Sodomites from the captivity of the four kings, Abraham is told not to be scared because the Lord is his shield (*Genesis* 15:1). Abraham is told this right after his success on the battlefield. Usually, a fighter would need to be told these words of confidence before going into battle, yet Abraham is told this after he has already won the battle. The Bible then continues with Abraham having his first revelation in Canaan, he is accredited with righteousness for trusting that his "seed" will be as numerous as the stars in the heavens (ibid 15:6), and then almost immediately Abraham seems to have a panic moment." How can I know that it <the land of Canaan> will be mine?" (ibid.15:8) He is scared he will not have a biological heir to inherit the land. Literally, in the passage before Abraham's land concern, he was credited with trusting in the Lord. Had he suddenly lost faith? After all, he was promised in (ibid.12:7)" I will give this land to your offspring" After which Abraham built an altar. If providing calm is the purpose of the Lord using the comment "fear not, I am your shield," then it certainly didn't work. Ironically, it seems, he only starts fearing once he is told not to fear.

Answer

When Abraham won the battle over the four kings and took back the captives, he then gave tithes for these captives and all other captured booty to Malchizedek. Abraham, according to Sumerian custom, thereby took total ownership of the population of Sodom. They are now his subjects. These people lost their freedom when they were taken captive by the four kings. In ancient Mesopotamia, the people who were taken as captives in war became slaves to the conquering nation. When Abraham captures them back, they become his captives/slaves. That might explain his mimicking Malchizedek's name for G-d. Abraham is not acting on his own behalf; he is representing these people, the Sodomites, whom he has taken possession of. They worshiped the Canaanite pantheon, where the chief god was *el*, as their representative. He invoked their language for god *(e-l elyon)* and did not use his monotheistic term.

As explained above, the Bible hinted via the story of Malchizedek that Abraham is the sovereign of Sodom. We will need this information so we can then answer our first question. What is the cause for the Biblical statement, Shall I hide from Abraham what I am going to do?"(*Genesis* 18:17).

The Sumerian temple priests were promoting the idea that they were able to interpret omens. When the magical omen foretold evil, the priest convinced the pagan worshipers and even the king himself that they could ward off its evil effect by preventive rites. (Daily Life in Ancient Mesopotamia, Karen Rhea Nemet-Nejat, Greenwood Press, pg. 198) The priests and the pagan gods would then rise in status by having the ability to protect their pagan supplicants from the evil foretold by the omens. By having the angels speak directly to the rightful sovereign, the Lord is showing the kings of Egypt and Mesopotamia that they should avoid the Temple and the pagan priesthood because they will get direct divine guidance and not need the priests to interpret omens.

As explained above, when the Bible hinted via the story of Melchizedek that Abraham is the sovereign of Sodom, we answered our first question. What is the cause for the Biblical statement, "Shall I hide from Abraham what I am going to do?" (*Genesis* 18:17).

Understanding that the Sumerian temple priests were promoting the idea that they could interpret omens. would explain why having the angels speak directly to the rightful sovereign, the kings of Egypt and Mesopotamia was an opportunity to avoid the Temple and the pagan priesthood. They became unnecessary because they were getting direct divine guidance and did not need the priests to interpret omens. Abraham, as the rightful king of the people of Sodom was worthy of receiving direct divine guidance and was told the fate of his sinning subjects.

Thus, there was a time in early earthly history, when the kings of the nations were told by dreams and angels of impending doom and disaster. We find at least three examples of this in *Genesis*. Here in the matter of Sodom, G-d tells his plans to Abraham, not the previous king, because as we stated above Abraham is the rightful sovereign of the Sodomites. The second example would be the dream communication given to Abimelech, king of Gerar after he kidnaps Sarah. This divine communication is similar to the third example when the Lord told Pharaoh (via the dreams of the fat and skinny cows) that a great famine was coming. This divine intervention was unique to its time and does not seem to occur after this period.

We can use Abraham's position visa-vie the Sodomites to answer our third question listed above why Abraham panicked after tithing the Sodom booty?." When G-d had promised Canaan to Abraham's "Zerah", which is translated as "seed." But according to Torah law, it has wider implications. This term includes those borne in Abraham's house i.e. offspring, slaves, as well as slaves, bought with cash from an outsider, who is not a descendant (ibid.17:12) which in Abraham's case might also have included the Sodomites since he did pay a tithe to Malchizedek. When Abraham realized that the Sodomites may fulfill the promise that the Lord had vowed to him that "your seed will inherit the land,", he began to panic. Abraham does not want the Sodomites to be included in the category of his "seed," thereby allowing them to inherit the land of Canaan.

Now it is clear why Abraham presses the Lord to confirm that his biological children will indeed inherit the land. A simple reading of the text would imply that he is afraid that his servant, Eliezer of Damascus would inherit. A careful reading would indicate that it is doubtful that Abraham fears that Eliezer might be the one to be his inheritor.

Scripture gives us a hint as to Abraham's real concerns by using the term "This will not be your heir"((ibid 15:4). In the previous sentence, Abraham was talking about his servant

Eliezer yet Scripture does not respond with "He will not be your heir" instead scripture records the term "this." By saying "This will not be your heir" instead of "he will not be your heir" we are led to other possibilities. We can conclude that Scripture is referring to a rejection of a group that would be legally entitled to inherit him. "This" must therefore refer to the "this" group of Sodomites that Abraham does not want to be included as his "Zerah."

Teacher's Notes for Chapter 2

Scripture relates that the King of Sodom tries to make a deal with Abraham, by saying, "You take the money, and I will take the people.." Abraham gives a hollow answer, "I don't want people to say that you made me wealthy."(*Genesis* 14:23). In fact, he was already wealthy from his interaction with the Egyptian King. The Bible relates how Abraham and Lot became so wealthy that they had to separate from each other because the local environment could not sustain the flocks of both Abraham and Lot. It is unlikely that anyone would say the King of Sodom made him rich. Abraham has ulterior reasons for not accepting the Sodomite King's terms. Abraham must have had reasons that he didn't decide to share with the king of Sodom.

Abraham's refusal to return the people of Sodom to their former king must be rooted in his mission to bring monotheism to Canaan. The ability for a person to discard the superstitious beliefs of paganism requires a combination of maturity and self-worth. We see from Abraham's efforts to secure freedom from captivity and political independence for the people of Sodom that he has a plan through which he expects them to eventually convert to monotheism. Conversion to monotheism requires a love for personal growth. The captives of Sodom, like all humans, experienced a cognitive leap as they went from captivity to freedom. This is the start of their journey to monotheism.

In addition, without a royal hierarchy, they had the opportunity to fulfill another ingredient to being primed for monotheism. Monotheism flourishes when people feel that they are not inferior to a ruling class. Although every society surely had leaders, Abraham made sure that there wasn't a hierarchical structure, i.e.. kings and nobles. This plan which was meant to lead Sodom to monotheism was based on Abraham's belief that people who recently achieved freedom and were not demoralized by being ruled by a monarchy would naturally accept monotheism.

We can now understand the Biblical sentence "I have given him special attention so that he will command his children and his household after him, and they will keep G-d's way, doing charity and justice. G-d will then bring about for Abraham everything he promised"* (*Genesis* 18:17). Prior to knowing that Abraham was the actual owner of the people of Sodom it was hard to understand why the angel is rambling on about the difference between these Sodomites and the children of Abraham. The answer is that once we see the parallels between the people of the *Exodus* and the people of Sodom, we can now fully understand what scripture is sharing with us. Both went from captivity to freedom, both were without a monarchy, just leaders. Yet the Israelites went on to monotheism, while the other was completely depraved. This is what the sentences (ibid.) are explaining to us. The power of freedom and equality only leads to monotheism when the people also take action. They must "do tzadakah" and justice.

Step-by-step Review of the Process for Achieving Abraham's Major Objective: Leading Canaan to monotheism.

What is preventing Abraham from returning these people to their former monarch? Why is he intent that there should not be a monarch over Sodom, who can claim sovereignty over them?

We begin our search for an answer by asserting that the Bible relates these dramatic stories for one reason. The stories reveal Abraham's methods and intentions to spread monotheism throughout Canaan. Here, the Bible is giving us a tactic that Abraham was testing to try to bring monotheism to Canaan.

Transforming the Sodomite Mindset

Abraham intends to employ a strategy that will help the newly freed Sodomites veer towards monotheism. The first step is to make sure the old king does not reign again over the Sodomites. The result of canceling the hierarchy is that it results in the people having a strong sense of self-worth. Without a noble class, people can view themselves as all being equal. Abraham expected that they would develop self-respect and turn away from self-abasing pagan practices.

The Strategy:

Abraham will arrange for these Sodomites to be independent of the monarchy.[1]

From archeology, we have discovered that the monarchs of Sumer continuously manipulated their subjects by using fear tactics. The goal of the fearmongering was to coerce the commoners to continue serving the Elites; they would warn the people that they would suffer the wrath of the gods if they failed to do so. The Bible tells us that Abraham believed that monotheism cannot begin with a superstitious population that is being manipulated by Elites. This would further explain why Abraham does not want to return the recaptured Sodomites to the original monarchy.

Thus far we have shown that the monotheistic mind, Abraham's creed, stood in opposition to the existing polytheistic culture. The Elites of polytheism did not want the masses to believe that the world was made for the benefit of humankind and that humanity could rise and seek an alternative to their fate. The Elites wanted to ensure that the masses stayed within the framework of polytheism and thereby remained submissive to their control.

We achieve the ideal world when there is a universal understanding that G-d has given humankind the gift of life and each individual has the innate power of finding meaning in this world. A world that was created for the specific purpose that humans can prosper.

When humans are being controlled and manipulated by the Elites, monotheism cannot take root. We can use this to explain why he did not want to return the people of Sodom to their king (see above) and was the basis of his teachings. His strategy was to pry the masses from the powerful grip of the Sumerian Elites by questioning the narrative that the Elites were promulgating. We find this challenge to the Elites in the alternative creation stories and in the subtle implementation of laws meant to pry away Abraham's followers from the grips of the Temple (see *The Genius of Abraham*, p. 68)

In addition, we find in the Torah that the Israelites carried this creed and culture, with them while they were enslaved in Egypt. These beliefs gave them dignity even under Egyptian slavery and kept them apart from the dazzling Egyptian polytheism. They knew they were the inheritors of the Abrahamic tradition. This tradition told all the Israelites that all humans are made in the image of G-d and they are all "equal before the Lord." This is what Korach was referring to when he claimed "All the people in the community are holy, and G-d is with them"(*Genesis*16:3). We also know that Abraham was adamant about not returning the captives of Sodom to the hierarchy (*Genesis* 14:23) as explained above. Based on these two references we can conclude that Abraham understood that a core belief of monotheism is that adherents trust that before G-d all people are equal and important.

Abraham must have expected the captives of Sodom to achieve monotheism. By preventing the previous king of Sodom from regaining the monarchy, combined with their recent freedom from captivity, Abraham created the fertile environment the Sodomites needed to achieve the ideal; they would naturally rise and become monotheistic.

With his mission always at the forefront of his actions, Abraham is determined to bring converts to monotheism. At the Brit Bain Habasorim, he understands that the people of Sodom are a test run for the experience the Israelites will endure in the future. They will be taken from slavery to freedom and like Sodom, they will not have a monarch, just a leader. When

Abraham is told that the experiment with Sodom has failed, he is assured that the Israelites will succeed.

The failure of Sodom is contrasted to the success that the Israelites will have in achieving monotheism because the Israelites are taught to take action. They will do "Tzadakah" and justice.[2]

Chapter Three:

The Seeming Israelite Obsession with Meat

Biblical Background

There are two times that the Israelites ask for meat. The first is in *Exodus* (16:2-13) and the second in *Numbers* (11:5-20). In *Exodus*, the Bible relates that the Israelites sang the "song of the sea", which gives thanks for their having safely crossed the parted Red Sea prior to the Egyptians drowning in the same sea. Yet shortly after this hymn of appreciation for G-d's protection, they are suddenly demanding meat. There aren't any negative responses from either G-d or Moses, and the meat is provided. They make a similar episode in *Numbers*, where the Israelites are demanding meat and threatening a return to Egypt. However this time there is a furious denunciation both by G-d and Moses against the Israelites for their requests.

Another dot to connect is at the time of the *Exodus*, the tenth plague brought upon the Egyptians the death of the firstborn. The Israelites are commanded, on the night of the tenth plague, to daub the blood of the Passover sacrifice on their doorposts and lintels to ensure that the punishment meant for the Egyptians didn't strike them as well. That night is also the night when they leave their Egyptian homes and begin their journey to Canaan. In describing the haste in which the *Exodus* happened the Bible tells us that the dough that was being prepared did not have time to rise before the Israelites were driven out of Egypt. The night of the *Exodus* followed the sacrificing and eating of the Pascal lamb. The dough that did not have time to rise was not for bread that was meant for the Pascal meal. Israelites would have had all day to prepare the bread for the Pascal meal. The Pascal lamb was slaughtered that afternoon and eaten that evening. After that, all preparations would have ceased. Another possibility for the Israelites baking bread in the middle of the night is that the Israelites needed the bread as provisions for the trip to Canaan. However, we know the bread was not being baked so the Israelites would have food for their way to Canaan because the Bible states clearly that the Israelites did not prepare provisions for the trip. (*Exodus* 12:39).

Questions

1. Accepting that the Israelites, who left Egypt and were slowly progressing toward Sinai were being guarded and cared for by angels, how could they have the audacity to make any further demands? They seem ungrateful and rebellious. Simultaneously, we are led to ask the obvious. What were the factors that allowed the Israelites to demand meat without recriminations in the *Exodus* episode? How did that differ from the similar request in *Numbers* 11:5?

2. Blood is a dirty, smelly medium that attracts flies and other insects. Why would the Israelites be commanded to engage in such odd behavior? Furthermore, why not just daub a tiny bit on the doorpost? Why was an application of blood on the lintel and both doorposts required?

3. Why are the Israelites baking bread in the middle of the same night that they were told to be ready for the exodus?

Answer

The Bible records that The Israelites knew they would be leaving Egypt soon after eating the Pascal meal. They were told to eat the Pascal meal shod and girded. The generation of the exodus understood their place in Jewish history. They knew they were the generation that G-d had promised to Abraham who would, after four hundred years of slavery, return to Canaan and claim their inheritance.

As explained in *The Genius of Abraham,* the Bris Bain Habasorim was a standard Suzerain-Vassal treaty that was common in Abraham's time. All such treaties consisted of six steps. The Israelites must have had a tradition that the returning generation would need to complete the Bris Bain Habasorim that Abraham did not complete. As per the Suzerain-Vassal Treaty, there were still three steps that still needed to be completed. They are as follows:

1. Both parties are required to walk between the split carcasses through a pathway that is delineated by animal blood on the tips of the carcasses. The Bible tells us that only the light and the cloud, representing the Lord walked down the aisle. Abraham neither delineated the split carcasses with blood nor did he walk down the aisle. These steps still need to be completed. The Israelites would need to daub the Pascal blood on their doorposts and lintel to mimic the pathway formed by the split carcasses. That explains the instruction to daub the blood on their doorways. The doorway would have symbolically fulfilled the daubing requirement of the Suzerain-Vassal Treaty.

2. The requirement that both parties walk the aisle of split carcasses would not be fulfilled until they walked through the split waters of the Reed Sea with full trust that G-d as their Suzerain, would protect them. This might explain why there was a spontaneous outpouring of emotion for crossing the Reed Sea, the Song of the Sea. We do not find similar exultation for the other heretofore miracles as the Bible does not indicate that the Israelites celebrated when each plague came upon the Egyptians but spared the Israelites. Crossing the Reed Sea was monumental to the Israelites because it completed another necessary step of the Suzerain-Vassal Treaty that even Abraham was unable to complete.

3. The last and final step of the s/v treaty is to share a meal with food supplied by both participants, That explains why they were baking bread on the night of the exodus. The Israelites would need to have bread for the feast that concludes the ceremony and finalizes the treaty. In fact, without this Brit meal, the deal is not concluded. It was for that decisive meal that they had a tradition of Abraham that when the redemption comes they would need to have bread ready.

Having a meal to finalize a covenant is not exclusive to this Suzerain-Vassal Treaty. We find an example of a covenant meal when Isaak and the king of Gerar (*Genesis* 26:30) made a covenant of peace. When Abraham previously made a similar treaty with the same King of Gerar the treaty was supposed to last for generations, yet Isaak is required to repeat it. This is because when the King of Gerar leaves before the meal is shared, the treaty is effectively canceled. The entire treaty needed to be redone with Isaak, but this time the concluding meal was shared by both parties.[3] The treaty is finally enacted.

When the Israelites saw they were lacking meat (for the menu, reference *(Genesis* 18:8) they cried for meat not because they were hungry for meat. They wanted the meat so they could have the meal that concludes the Suzerain-Vassal Treaty and guarantee their right to Canaan. Thus, they did not get any objection to that noble objective.

Teacher's Notes for Chapter 3: A Passover Thought

The Haggadah quotes Scripture that every generation must see itself as the generation going out of Egypt. The obvious questions are:

If a person has never been to Egypt and has never been a slave how could they see themselves as leaving Egypt?

Why does the text begin with the wording "every generation" when it could simply begin with the part of the sentence stating that every person must see himself as leaving Egypt? To answer these questions, we can simply say that a person is not being asked to imagine himself as leaving Egypt but we are being asked to adopt the mindset of those who went out. The exiting Israelites were told by Moses and were shown signs to alert them to the exodus. We know those Israelites who participated in the exodus were aware of their place in Jewish history. They became the generation whom Abraham was told at the BBH (Brit Bain Habasorim) would leave the land of their oppression to go to claim the land of Canaan. So scripture is telling us that every Jew must see himself at the Seder as aware of the part his/her generation plays in Jewish destiny, just as that Jewish generation who long ago left Egypt. We are asked to see our generation's role as a cog in the grand tapestry of Jewish destiny. Even while we sit at the Seder table eighty years after the holocaust and seventy-five years after the creation of the state of Israel we are asked to be part of the links of Jewish history. Although we were not actually at the Exodus, we can still view ourselves as having shared values and generational awareness with the Jewish people's greatest generation that went from Slavery to Freedom. With this in mind, we can now explain why Scripture begins the sentence with "Every generation." Just like the generation of the Exodus, later generations are obligated to identify their place in the chain of Jewish history, and each individual is expected to be a vital part of a generation, and that generation, in turn, is commanded to link itself to the Jewish people's greatest generation.

Chapter Four:

Abraham–Moses Connection

Biblical Background

The Bible records several of the challenges Abraham encountered in Canaan. Soon after the Bris Milah, Abimelech, king of Gerar, (*Genesis* 20:2) kidnaps Sari and he and all his subjects are punished with the inability to produce children. Scripture says that Abraham prayed for him and his people and they were all healed. The reader could consider that this story shows us that Abraham used the power of prayer to achieve specific outcomes. This incident occurs after the dramatic destruction of Sodom, where Abraham was unable to prevent their annihilation. This difference in Abraham's ability to affect outcomes was discernible. When Abraham prayed to his G-d for Gerar's healing he was able to obtain a positive outcome. This was surely noted by the denizens of Gerar.

Four hundred years later, when Moses accepted to lead the Israelites from Egypt. He asks G-d to provide him with something to prove to the people that he is there to lead them out of Egypt in fulfillment of the promise made to Abraham at the Bris Bain Habasorim. G-d then proceeds to give him three signs with which to convince the Israelites. They are as follows:

1. A pitcher of water is turned into blood.

2. Moses is able to suddenly cause leprosy to infect his hand and then immediately make the skin heal.

3. His staff changes to a snake and back again.

Soon after the Israelites crossed the sea and sang the "song of the sea." They are unable to find potable water until the water is supplied by a miracle the Lord then tells the people "I am the Lord your healer"(*Exodus* 15:26).

Three Questions

1. Within one chapter, we find that Abraham tries to convert two groups of pagans, the people of Gerar and the people of Sodom. When Abraham prays for Abimelech and his people of Gerar he is able to achieve a successful outcome, yet when he advocates for Sodom he must negotiate a deal that ultimately fails to save Sodom. How are we to make a distinction between

Abraham's approach to helping Abimelech and his failed efforts to save Sodom?

2. Why is Moses given these three particular signs to prove that he was sent from the Lord to free the Israelites from bondage? Egypt was a land where magicians had a central role in the running of the country. Surely these "signs" were not going to impress the Israelites or their Egyptian enslavers.

3. When the Lord tells the people " I am the Lord your healer" Israelites were seeking to slake their thirst, they were not seriously sick, Why does the Lord identify himself as their "healer"?

Answer

In Sumerian culture, each god only had only one realm. When Abraham prayed for Abimelech, the people of Gerar thought that he was answered by his G-d, who, according to the Sumerian culture, must have been the God of healing. Therefore, Moses is given signs that relate to healing because that is what the god of Abraham was known as and that is what his descendants would have recognized as a hint of divine attention. Thus, all these signs: The healing of leprosy, the turning of water to blood, and having dominance over the symbol of healing, the snake. These symbols would have been meaningful to the Israelites who were still influenced by polytheistic culture and possibly identified their G-d as having one special power. Eventually, at the first interaction the Israelites have with the Lord after the crossing of the Red Sea, he introduces himself as "your healer", the very attribute they would have known Him by.

We can discern Israel's interest in the appropriate name of Abraham's G-d from the verses in the "Song of the Sea." In the midst of praising G-d for the miracle of the crossing there is a sentence that seems incongruous, After using the name Yud Kai Vov Kai in the first two sentences the third sentence finally says, " G-d is the master of war, Yud-Kai-Vav-Kai is his name (*Exodus* 15:3). The order of the sentences should be to first identify the name of the protagonist. That third sentence should be the first sentence. What are we to deduce from this? The simplest answer is to apply the knowledge we learned about Sumerian paganism namely: the god of war is not the god of healing. Each god had a unique domain. This pagan idea seems to be found in many pagan cultures. With that Egyptian pagan influence, we read that they immediately give praise to the war G-d of Moses but still do not recognize this "power" as the same G-d that was Abraham's healing G-d. Even though the song uses the term "My father's God, I will exalt Him" (ibid.15:2). This reference to "father's G-d" may refer to the war god that guided Abraham to win his war against the four kings in the battle to recapture Sodom and his nephew Lot.

Thus, it seems that there is some evidence that even after the crossing of the sea the Israelites are awaiting the healing god of Abraham to bring them to Canaan. They are finally told in the very next story after the Song of the Sea, at the bitter waters of Marah, "I am G-d who heals you (ibid.15:26). This sentence is imperative to the narrative because it finally identifies the protagonist as the healing G-d of Abraham. The Israelites are ready to follow through on the promises made to Abraham at the Bris Bain Habasorim, complete the missing steps, and proceed to accept their inheritance, the land of Canaan.

Teacher's Notes for Chapter 4

It is always interesting to see the symmetry in the biblical narrative. Above we have read that the exodus and the Israelite's travel to Sinai contained elements of a homage to Abraham and his actions at the BBH. This would be an appropriate time to look for the symmetrical homage to Abraham at the end of their journey and as expected it is found just before they end their wanderings and are about to enter Canaan. The King of Moab brings Bilom to curse the nation although they have already passed the land of Moab. So why is there an immediacy for Bilom to curse the Israelites who are no longer a threat to Moab? The answer can be found in the geography of the Dead Sea.

The Israelites have camped at a spot, across the Jordan from Jericho, called the western plains of Moab, (*Numbers* 22:1). Archeologists have determined that this is the same location where Sodom once stood (Biblical Archaeology Review, March/April 2013). We already established (see chapter 2) that Abraham was the nominal king of Sodom and the Bible tells us that he was unable to save them from their fate. Now at, Kikar Hayarden, in the very place where Abraham failed to influence the incorrigible Sodom stands the dignified children of Abraham standing under the glory of the Lord and ready to collect their inheritance. We have a hint to this when camped at Kikar Hayarden, the Jews are given two commandments. They are told, that once the land is conquered they are required to establish the cities of the Levites and the cities of refuge.

Why are these specific commandments given here? Once again we see the homage to Abraham, these two kinds of cities align with the statements made by Abraham's visitors at Mamre. The angels who visited Abraham at Mamre differentiated the failed Sodomites from Abraham's children. The reason for this different outcome was that Abraham taught his children to walk in the ways of the Lord to "do tzedakah" and justice (*Genesis* 18:17). Hence, the Jews are given the instruction to build the cities of refuge as an example of the Jewish people's system of justice.

The cities of the Levites are an example of "do tzedakah." To explain this we need to go back to the pagan Sumerian Elites were able to keep their grip on power because they taught their citizens that the land belonged to the gods and humans were only given access to the land as long as they worshiped the gods correctly. The Torah, in contrast, is saying that because of the Brit Bain Habasorim, the land belongs to Abraham's progeny and therefore they are doing an act of tzadakah when they give the Levite a city. Similarly, when they create a city of refuge they are doing justice. Standing in the same place where Sodom once stood the children of Abraham are prepared to do tzadakah and justice, just like the angels at Mamre said.

By standing at Kikar Hayarden, prior to entering Canaan, the Israelites remember both the failure to save Sodom and how it turned into a blessing by replacing the flawed Sodomites with Abraham's progeny. Thus, the beginning of the exodus (i.e.. The Israelites baking bread on the night of Passover) and the end of the *Exodus* as explained above is an homage to our father Abraham, the Bris Bain Habasorim he prepared and his visitors at Mamre.

Chapter Five:

Brit Bain Habasorim (BBH)–Brit Milah (*Genesis*:15,16,17)

Biblical Background

After rescuing Sodom from the Four Kings, Abraham is suddenly concerned that he will not have children to inherit the blessings that G-d had given him. When G-d assures him that he will indeed have biological children to inherit his blessings. Abraham immediately trusts that this will happen. However, he quickly voices a different concern. Abraham wants a formal acknowledgment that the land of Canaan will be his and will be given to his children as an inheritance.

Abraham is living his life deeply influenced by Sumerian culture. Another example of this influence is the importance of having a male heir. Being concerned about a formal land transfer would be typical for a Sumerian living in the time of Abraham. Numerous tablets and stela have been found delineating boundaries showing us that in Sumeria the people were very conscious of land, boundaries, and preserving legal title. It is therefore not surprising that Abraham would be inclined to seek that G-d formally transfer the land of Canaan to his progeny. Since this is not done in corporeal courts but takes place while Abraham is in a deep trance we must accept that Abraham, heavily influenced by Sumerian culture, is concerned about a land transfer without a formal land treaty. Abraham was concerned the land transfer would not be recognized as legally binding for future generations. G-d loves Abraham but will that love last an eternity? Abraham was aware of the rise and fall of the Sumerian city-states. He wanted the reward of Canaan to be irrevocable. G-d agrees and the Brit Bain Habasorim (BBH) is G-d's response to Abraham's concerns.

G-d tells Abraham that they will enact a customary land transfer agreement of the time, the Suzerain-Vassal Treaty, which will guarantee the land transfer to Abraham and his progeny for eternity.

Following this treaty we read of Sarah providing Abraham with her handmaid, Hagar, as a child-making concubine. Sarah then turns on Hagar resulting in her running away. Hagar has an encounter with an angel whom she labels as the "seeing god" and returns to Abraham's camp.

It is after this incident that the Bible records the Brit Milah, a treaty between G–d and Abraham where Abraham receives blessings and is directed that he, his household, and all males in future generations must be circumcised. When Abraham is told that Sarah will bear Isaak, he is skeptical that as aged parents they can still bear children. Abraham then says to G-d" May it be granted that Ishmael live before you." G-d then proceeds to give Ishmael one of the incentives that was originally given to Abraham to leave Haran; the blessing of "becoming a great nation." Although ninety-nine years old Abraham circumcises himself, his household and, even Ishmael.

Questions

1. At the first Brit (BBH) Abraham is assured that he will have many children, like the stars in the night sky, and the land of Canaan is transferred to Abraham and his progeny. When the Brit Milah is suddenly made, the same blessings of biological children and inheriting the land of Canaan are repeated. Why does G-d make a second Brit with Abraham?

2. At both Britot the Bible in a rare revelation tells us what Abraham's thoughts were at the time. At the BBH he is credited with righteousness for trusting that G-d will greatly multiply his progeny. At the Brit Milah, he thinks both he and Sarah are too old for childbearing. Abraham is doubtful that his dream to have a child with Sarah will ever happen. Where did his trust in the Lord go?

3. The Bible gives us the story of Hagar between the two Britot. Hagar is running away from what she views as an abusive mistress. Although Sarah had initially raised Hagar up from the status of a handmaiden to become Abraham's concubine, Sari seems to suddenly turn on Hagar. The Bible seemingly attributes it to Hagar lauding her pregnancy over barren Sarah. Surely Sarah expected Hagar to bear Abraham a child, after all, wasn't that the purpose of making her Abraham's concubine? Some lauding would be normal behavior. What triggers Sari to hate Hager so much?

Answer

During this epoch, it was common for a Suzerain to offer the use of land to a Vassal in exchange for the Vassal showing allegiance and fealty to the Suzerain. Archeologists have found several written examples of this Suzerain-Vassal Treaty. The Brit (covenant) that transfers the land of Canaan to the children of Abraham follows the same pattern of other Suzerain-Vassal treaties. Often prior to the actual treaty, the suzerain would commonly request an agreement or alliance with a Vassal and then proceed to qualify the Vassal before the formal establishment of a permanent treaty (J.M. Durand, in L. De Meyer et al.(eds) Fragmenta Historiae Elamicae (Paris, Editions Recherches sur les Civilisations, A.D.P.F.1986pg115-116). The BBH (Brit Bain Habasorim) was therefore just an agreement prior to the actual treaty. So while it might look like there are two Covenants, it is actually one. What we have is one treaty with the BBH almost like a preamble agreement to the actual Brit. It introduces the participants, provides previous contacts between the parties, lays out the expectation of the Suzerain, and implies the subjugation of the Vassal by condemning his children to four hundred years of slavery.[4] The final details of the agreement, which all covenants require, were made at the Brit Milah. The fourteen years that separate the two Covenants must have acted as a testing phase to see if the conditions of the BBH were held up. This process of first testing the initial treaty prior to finalization was not uncommon.

Unfortunately, things did not go as planned and Abraham failed to even convert all the members of his own household, i.e., Hagar and Ishmael. Following the Biblical style, we must suss out Abraham's failure from the Hagar story since Abraham is never recorded in the text as having failed. At the Brit Milah, we are told that Abraham's mission is modified. G-d did not cancel the transfer of Canaan to Abraham, however the terms were changed. The scope of Abraham's primary objective was reduced from striving for the universal adoption of monotheism to just his "seed" accepting monotheism. In addition, a qualification of circumcision was now required for the fulfillment of the covenant. These blessings began as inducements to leave Haran and were slowly turned into blessings as the Britot progressed.

Abraham continued his life's work in Canaan. This included several evangelical efforts against polytheism (see chapter 7). The Brit Milah which as we stated above is followed by the testing of the viability of the (BBH). The Bible gives us only one example of Abraham's proselytizing efforts in Canaan during the testing phase and sadly it is of Abraham's failure. That failure was in his very own household. In Summary, Abraham enters into the BBH, the Brit is tested, he cannot make headway with converting the Canaanites as exemplified by the Hagar and Ishmael remaining polytheistic. His mission is changed at the Brit Milah.

Once we know that Hagar remained an incorrigible pagan we then know why the BBH needed to be modified. We know that Hagar remained a pagan from the following archaeological revelation; In ancient Mesopotamia, each god was given a separate domain for example there was a god of earth and a separate god of water. Now we can understand why we are told the Hagar story. The Bible never calls Abraham's efforts to convert the Canaanites a failure but alludes to it by giving us just one example of Abraham's efforts that occurred after the BBH (Bris Bain Habasorim). That example is the story about, Hagar, his concubine. Hagar was given to Abraham as a baby-making concubine by barren Sari. She runs away from Sarah whom she claims is oppressing her. Hagar tells all this to the angel who then assures her of blessings and directs her to return to Sarah. Hagar then calls to the angel "You are the god of seeing"(*Genesis* 16:13). In monotheism, there isn't room for a "god of seeing." That idea that G-d is restricted to only one domain, in this case, "seeing", is a polytheistic view of how the gods rule the earth. As stated above, the Mesopotamian pagans believed that every god had a unique domain i.e.. land, sea, harvest, war, etc. This is in contrast to monotheism where the universe is created and guided by one spiritual G-d. This monotheistic belief is confirmed by the Bible when we are given Abraham's description of a similar encounter with an angel. After the Binding of Isaak Abraham names the place of the

Binding "the place where the Lord will be seen"(*Genesis* 22:14) Abraham does not try to give the Lord any anthropomorphic qualities. As a monotheist, he only expresses a future where the Lord can be "seen" by His wonders that He will perform on this mountain or He will be "seen, as their G-d, by those who will worship Him on the mountain (Rashi). We can now see that Abraham was unable to convert Hagar. This failure symbolized why the entire mission needed to be modified. Brit Milah gives the new terms of Abraham's mission. Abraham will limit his missionary efforts to keeping his clan monotheistic. He and his children will receive the land of Canaan only on conditions.

Now we can answer our third question as to why Sari hated her. Hagar refused to give up her polytheistic views even while living in Abraham's very house as his baby-making concubine. Sarah as the mother of monotheism found this lack of awareness intolerable.

This realization of failure affected Abraham severely. This is revealed to us by the Bible telling us Abraham's private thoughts. At the BBH he is optimistic and self-confident, he believes the prophecy that his seed will be as numerous as the stars in the sky. However, after failing to convert Hagar, Abraham loses his optimism and by the Brit Milah, he projects his sense of failure onto the prophecy that he will have a child with Sarah. His grand mission to bring the world monotheism is failing in Canaan; even Hagar, his baby-making concubine has remained a polytheist. We have thus answered the second question: What happened to Abraham's faith? When G-d tells him of the upcoming birth of Isaak, Abraham questions the possibility as he projects his own sense of failure even on G-d's revelation of the birth of a child. He says that due to his own and Sarah's age, the birth will not happen. We can relate this to similar emotions we find even today in modern times. Despondent people tend to project a negative outlook on the world that is full of failed expectations. We have now laid the groundwork to answer our first question.

At the Brit Milah, G-d abruptly changes Abraham's mission. It was no longer Abraham's mission to convert the entire Canaan and introduce their inhabitants to monotheism, he was just to have his family, his nation in the covenant (baini ubaincha).[5] Once again. As stated above, by knowing a little about ancient Mesopotamian culture we understood that Hagar remained a practicing idolatress. With that, we were able to answer the first question. A second Brit, the Brit Milah, was required because it changed Abraham's mission from converting all of Canaan to just maintaining his family as monotheists. When Sarah realized that Hagar could not be converted she grew to hate her.

The parable about Hagar is important to understanding the need for a second Brit. The Bible is actually giving us an indication of why the second Brit was necessary. Scripture reveals that Abraham was failing to convert the Canaanites. We are told this indirectly by being told that he could not even influence members of his own family. By understanding that at the Brit Milah, Abraham's mission is changed from a universal mission to a parochial mission. Under the revised Brit, he is required to influence just his own family as the Bible writes the treaty is made "Banai Ubaincha"(between me and you). Once again, by knowing the Sumerian culture and how they structured their legal agreements, we as modern readers can better understand the Biblical narrative.

The Brit Milah gave a very different outlook on Abraham's mission in Canaan than the BBH originally did. It did not cancel or override the BBH. We see the continuation of the BBH at the Brit Milah when Abram and Sari are given new names The changing of names was per the requirements of the Suzerain-Vassal Treaty (for a listing of all requirements see the chapter on Suzerain-Vassal Treaty). This continuation of the Pro-forma details showed Abraham that they are still considered vassals to the Suzerain, G-d, with whom they have the BBH agreement. Therefore Abraham also knows that his zera (seed) will proceed to "a land not theirs" and needs to prepare them with guidance that will allow them to survive intact.

Eventually, we will reveal that the entire section of the Bible from Abraham preparing the split carcasses to his sacrificing a ram in place of his son is actually one long legal document that allows us to answer several difficult questions within the text.

Here are two examples:

1. The word "Tzadaka" is used both as a noun and as a verb, When used as a noun 15:6 the text states that Abraham's trust in the Lord is credited for "Tzadaka." Later on in chapter 18:19, Abraham's children are differentiated from the people of Sodom because they do "Tzadaka."Here the term Tzadaka is used as a verb. The multiple uses of the term are now easily explained. At the beginning of every legal document, there is a definition of terms. In Chapter 15:6 the text defines the term "Tzadaka." It is a quality of his character that Abraham exhibited when he unreservedly trusted that ultimately G-d would bestow upon him the progeny he desperately sought. When Abraham's children are instructed to follow the Lord's way by doing "Tzadakah" we are to understand that the Bible is telling us that we must live our lives with the same unreserved trust that Abraham had. This is one of the pillars of monotheism and the foundation upon which the rest of the Torah follows.

2. Knowing that we are actually looking at a legal contract for the transfer of the land of Canaan in the form of a Suzerain-Vassal Treaty we can explain why we have the name changes for both Abraham and Sarah and why we needed to have a Brit Milah in addition to the BBH.

Teacher's Notes for Chapter 5: Keeping lists

Archeologists have concluded from the plethora of recorded tablets that the Sumerians were ardent list keepers and similarly, we find many lists in the Bible. By analyzing the changes in the lists, we can learn the movement of the Biblical narrative. The three lists relevant to Abraham are:

1. The inducements that are given to Abraham to leave Haran.

2. The inducements that are given to Isaak not to leave Canaan for Egypt.

3. The blessings that are given to Abraham at the Brit Milah and after the Binding of Isaak.

By analyzing the inducements given to Isaak to stay in Canaan we can clearly see the movement from Abraham's initial mission of converting the entire world to monotheism, change to a narrower parochial mission of establishing a monotheistic nation that stems from Abraham's "zerah (seed)."

There were seven inducements that G-d gave to Abraham to get him to leave Haran and there were six inducements given to Isaak to stay in Canaan and not leave for Egypt during a Canaanite famine. Finally, there are a total of seven blessings given to Abraham; five were given at the Brit Milah and two at the Binding of Isaak.

When we examine the inducements given to Abraham to leave Haran we note the universality of the inducements and how they imply that Abraham's message will be spreading to the whole world " I will bless those who bless you and he who curses you, I will curse. All the families of the earth will be blessed through you"(*Genesis* 12:3). When these inducements to leave, Haran are compared to the actual blessings given to Abraham at the Brit Milah and the Binding of Isaak the change in scope is discernible but not yet obvious. However, when we read of the inducements given to Isaak not to leave Canaan, we can clearly see how the mission shifted from the original universal mission to just a parochial mission that focused on the nation of Abraham. "I will make your descendants as numerous as the stars of the sky and grant them all these lands. All the nations on earth shall be blessed through your descendants" (*Genesis* 26:4)

When the inducements were given to Isaak, they were made to him after the Brit Milah was concluded with his father. By noting the subtle changes in terminology, we saw the movement away from a universal mission to a restricted mission.

This sharp contrast between the two sets of inducements. The universal scope of the inducements presented to Abraham to leave Haran was changed to a more personal, narrower scope of inducements offered to Isaak not to leave Canaan. We already saw a narrowing of the scope when Abraham is told at the Brit Milah the term "between me and you" and we are seeing the narrower scope repeated and confirmed with Isaak's inducements to stay in Canaan.

Abraham's mission in Sumer and Haran changed when he relocated to Canaan. The Israelites are to stand apart, in their own land, from the rest of the world. Israel's *reason d'etre* is to have a bond with G-d, not to directly influence the rest of the world. Ultimately, the nations of the world will look to Israel and bless their own children by saying may you be like an Israelite. Thereby using Israel as a standard as to what is considered humanity's highest level of morality, achievement & spiritual connectivity (Rashi, *Genesis* 26:4).

Chapter Six:

Brit Bain Habasorim–Brit Milah, Binding of Isaak

Biblical Background

After the Brit Milah the Bible records several stories that led up to the Binding of Isaak. One story was the eviction of Hagar and Ishmael from Abraham's camp after Sarah caught Ishmael continuing to worship idols. Abraham is concerned about taking such extreme measures, but after consulting directly with the Lord he proceeds with the eviction. The result of the eviction is that Ishmael only inherited the promises made to him at the Brit Milah, however, he does not get any part of Canaan.

Immediately after the Brit Milah, the text returns us to the tragic story of Sodom, where Abraham tries to negotiate a reprieve from their imminent destruction but even after making his best effort to save them, he is ultimately, unable to prevent their ultimate doom.

Another story is about Abimelech, King of Gerar, who kidnaps Sarah for his Harem. When a curse of sickness befalls himself and his people, he receives a heavenly directive to return her to Abraham. He is also told to ask Abraham to pray on his behalf to heal his kingdom's malady from the curse. Abraham prays and Abimelech and his people are healed. Abimelech gives Abraham a hefty gift for helping to heal the effects of the curse. He also suggests to Abraham that they formalize a multi-generational treaty. Without providing any details we know the treaty doesn't happen. We deduce the treaty failed because scripture records, in a later Chapter, that Isaak made the same multi-generational treaty with Abimelech. If there was already a multi-generational treaty made with Abraham in place another treaty with Isaak would not have been necessary.

Each of the three stories records another setback that Abraham suffered since the Brit Milah.

Within this series of setbacks is also recorded a highlight of Abraham's life - the birth, circumcision, and naming of Isaak. Sarah catches Ishmael in pagan worship, as Isaak's weaning is being celebrated. Sadly, this leads to the eviction of Ishmael and Hagar. Even the great joy of the birth and weaning of Isaak is not perfect but tempered by the eviction of another beloved child.

"After these things, the Lord tests Abraham" with the Binding of Isaak (*Genesis* 22:1). After Abraham passes the test, he sacrifices a ram he finds caught in a hedge and receives the last two blessings. It is important to note that the final blessing bestowed on Abraham was that the "world will be blessed through Abraham's seed." This blessing was one of the inducements originally told to Abraham at the very beginning of his mission and only became part of the covenant here, at the very end. This inducement helped to inspire Abraham to leave Haran, yet it was not mentioned in either the Brit Milah or the Brit Bain Habasorim blessings. However, once Abraham triumphs at the Binding of Isaak this blessing is bestowed (*Genesis* 22:18). An additional blessing is also given; the land of Canaan will be inherited with intact cities.

After the Binding of Isaak, Abraham, and Isaak do not return to Sarah, who is living in Hebron. Instead, they go to Bear Sheva. Scripture does point out the great efforts Abraham extends to bury Sarah with dignity.

Questions

After Hagar and her son are evicted and several other events, Abraham is tested with the "Binding of Isaak." At the time of the testing, the Brit Milah had already been completed. Abraham had already been promised the land of Canaan. If the purpose of the testing is to confirm Abraham's faith, then the testing should have happened before entering into the covenant. Before entering an agreement with a Vassal, the Suzerain would normally make sure the Vassal is vetted yet the Torah clearly writes." After these things G-d tests Abraham.." Why test after the covenant is signed sealed and delivered?

2. After Abraham champions the test of the Binding of Isaak he is told" Now I know you fear me. "We have other examples where we say Abraham loved G-d (Isaiah 41:8). Why does the text focus on Abraham showing that *he* fears the Lord, instead of saying, "Now I know you love me"? Additionally, we know that G-d told the Avos "not to fear." Each one of the forefathers is given a personal directive not to fear: Abraham *Genesis* 15:1,

Isaak *Genesis* 26:24, and Jacob *Genesis* 28:15. Why is G-d, at the binding of Isaak, suddenly seeking for Abraham to fear him?

3. As a reward for his triumph at the trial of the Binding of Isaak, Abraham is told that when his children get the land of Canaan, it will come with an upgrade of already built cities. Why was the blessing of Canaan coming with pre-built cities, a feature that was never mentioned before, now included in the blessing?

Answer

In Sumer, Abraham was fighting for an urban population to move away from polytheistic temples. These temples were staffed by priests who influenced simple minded people to believe they were created for the sole purpose of serving the Elites. The Elites consisted of the nobility and the priestly caste. They built awe-inspiring Ziggurats using newly developed burnt brick technology. These massive building projects along with impressive canal networks were used to guarantee that the population stayed enthralled and submissive to the Elites. At Canaan, Abraham is facing a very different venue. The population is comparatively rural with few city/states. Here the worship of idolatry is endemic to the population and is not imposed from a calculating Elite class. Abraham tried several methods to influence the pagans of Canaan, but they all ended in failure. We can see Abraham's failure to attract converts in Canaan when he needed to amass an army to combat the four Kings who conquered and seized the residents of Sodom. His entire army was a very small number of only 312 soldiers, and as stated in scripture this army was drawn from his household. Abraham, fails in Canaan, to attract many followers and even fails to convert members of his own household. As scripture indicates Hagar and Ishmael remain polytheistic.

The Binding of Isaak will test if Abraham is failing due to the overwhelming attraction of Canaanites to idolatry, or if he is failing because he lacks conviction for the cause. He will be challenged to prove that he is indeed an obedient devotee of monotheism and consequently, he can reassure himself of his obedience to G-d and reverse his sadness. [6]The test begins, and Abraham is called by his new name and responds Hineni.[7]We can see that this test was designed for Abraham's benefit because God's request begins with the words "Please take your son." That is followed with, Lech Lacha (go for you), the same term that was used when the Lord induced Abraham to leave Haran (Lech Lacha, Rashi (*Genesis* 12:1) identifies this term as a way of saying "go for your own benefit." Here Abraham's progeny is in mortal danger yet the "go-for you" term is still used implying for your benefit. How can the death of a child be called for your benefit? "For you" must imply that this task was to help Abraham accomplish a personal matter and the health of his child was not in danger.

Once we understand that Abraham was suffering from the sadness that results from repeated failures, we can then make sense of all this. As humans, we can see how passing a trial could begin the healing process. At no time should we think that G-d actually wanted Abraham to sacrifice Isaak. Scripture is clear from the start of the Chapter by stating that "the Lord tested Abraham." These words tell us that all that was to follow was only to uplift Abraham and not to destroy Isaak.

Humanity was at a turning point. Sumer was the first civilization since the Great Flood and God had invested in Abraham to lead the world back to monotheism. Taking Abraham out of Haran and giving him and his children, the land of Canaan was a gesture that stopped the good work Abraham was doing in Sumer and had him try to repeat his success in Canaan. Thus, Abraham's failure to convert the Canaanites and his subsequent sadness was something that needed immediate attention. Abraham's recovery was essential since there was much work still to accomplish. Primarily, Abraham needed to prepare Isaak to guide and influence future generations. They needed tools to survive their time "in a foreign land that is not theirs for 400 years." Maybe that is why the Bible states that after the trial Abraham does not return to Sarah at Hebron, but he goes with his son to a place where he will focus on educating and influencing Isaak, the rural town of Bear Sheva. We have now answered the first question- Why test Abraham after he was already in the covenant? The short answer is that it was not a test of his faith instead it was a method to heal him from the sadness of repeated failures.

By knowing about ancient Sumerian Temple practices, we can answer the second question. Although there is extensive proof that the Bible is intensely interested in creating a society of devoutly religious & engaged individuals. At the same time, we are commanded to serve G-d via the emotion of "love." This is in contrast to the priests and elites of Sumer who used "fear" to subjugate the pagans. When Abraham is told, "Now I know you fear me" the Bible is speaking in the colloquial; "fear" was the common Sumerian term for worship. At that time the Temples engendered "fear" to get the pagans to respond to their demands. Thus, the words fear and worship became interchangeable. A pagan feared the gods. Oblations, according to pagan faith, were brought so the gods would not seek to destroy mankind. The priests told the Canaanites salvation comes only when the worshiper followed a very specific set of rituals whose protocols were only known to the priesthood.

When the angel says to Abraham at the Binding of Isaak, "Now I see that you fear him"(*Genesis* 22:12), it cannot mean Abraham serves G-d out of fear, since as a monotheist, Abraham worships G-d out of love. By applying our knowledge of Sumerian expression, it actually implies a different meaning. The verse is saying, "Now I know you worship G-d <and trust him> that you have not withheld your only son from him.' This is the result that Abraham was waiting for. Now he can be sure that the problem with converting the Canaanites is with the incorrigible people of Canaan, and not with himself. Abraham is thus healed from his sadness, knowing that the reason for his inability to influence Canaan was because of their obdurate paganism and not because of any flaw within himself.

Again, by knowing Sumerian traditions we can answer the third question. Under Sumerian law when a person is put through a trial by an accuser and is proven a champion he is entitled to an award. Here G-d gives Abraham his reward based on Abraham's own values. Abraham seeks a world that will be a better place for all mankind. G-d uses the Binding of Isaak as an opportunity to support Abraham's quest by blessing him that the whole world will be blessed through his children. This was the same incentive given to Abraham when he left Haran, (12:1-3) but this blessing was not given at the BBH nor at Brit Milah only now does it become part of the final Brit. There was an additional upgrade as an award for passing the test. The promise of Abraham receiving the land of Canaan, which was given at the BBH, and Brit Milah, was now given an upgrade. The blessing that the land will come with cities. It was part of Sumerian culture that city living was more important than nomadic living. This is another example that Abraham was culturally Sumerian.

Teacher's Notes for Chapter 6

Just prior to the Brit Milah, the Lord says "Abraham Walk before Me and be perfect. I will make my covenant Banai Ubaincha <between me and you>" (*Genesis* 17:1). We do not find Abraham's verbal response to the change in Abraham's mission." Abram fell on his face" (ibid.17:3) This modification in the mission from a universal conversion to monotheism to Banai Ubaincha. Abraham accepts this contraction in his mission without comment.

G-d proceeds to change Abraham's and Sari's names. This change of the names is significant because it is the next step in the Suzerain-Vassal Treaty. This gives Abraham a renewed sense of confidence. G-d is foretelling he will succeed in this revised mission and that he will be able to spread monotheism within his own family. Finally, we hear Abraham's response to the mission's revision: "May it be granted that Ishmael live before you."

These enigmatic words have been explained by commentaries to mean that Abraham is saying that having Ishmael as my son is sufficient and it is not necessary for Sari to also have a son.

With the understanding that there has been a modification in the treaty for Canaan, we read an entirely different meaning of this verse. Abraham is pointing the finger at Ishmael as the cause for his mission's contraction. He is actually pleading that although Ishmael is guilty of idol worship, and exemplified the failure of Abraham to convert Canaan, he should be granted life and not be punished for his pagan worship.

The Bible hints at this analysis by making a special citation of Ishmael's circumcision (*Genesis* 17:25) This seems to be a superfluous sentence. Abraham was already commanded to circumcise all the males of his household, which surely would have included Ishmael. Why would it be necessary to have a separate sentence to point out that Ishmael was circumcised?

Maybe the Bible is sharing with us that Abraham circumcises even Hagar's child; whom Abraham was fully aware was a pagan. Being a committed pagan would have excluded him from the covenant.

This action shows that Abraham has his old confidence restored and believes that he will inspire all his children to be monotheists.

That wishful thinking is short-lived since once Isaak is born Hagar's son is caught worshiping idols "and Sarah saw the son of Hagar the Egyptian.... making merry"(*Genesis* 21:9). Making merry is a euphemism for idol worship (Rashi) and Sarah insists on getting both Ishmael and Hagar out of the house. After conferring with G-d, something that Sarah has been angrily asking for prior to the Brit Milah. "May the Lord judge between me and you" (*Genesis* 16:5) Abraham is now told that he must accept that Hagar and Ishmael will never convert to monotheism.

This inability of the Canaanites to move away from idolatry may have been the reason why Abraham later insisted that Isaak's wife not be a Canaanite.

Chapter Seven:

Sarah, the Mother of the Jewish People

Part One: Reviewing the Source Material

Biblical Reference:

We find stories in the Torah that when simplistically read seem to be at odds with the ethics of the Torah.

The two stories of Abraham colluding with Sarah to hide their marital status are examples of this anomaly. Scripture quotes Abraham telling Sarah that the reason for this deception- if Sarah was known to be married to him the Elites would kill Abraham and take Sarah to the king's harem.

Abraham proceeds to lay out his plan; they need to say they are siblings instead of revealing their true marital status. Ultimately, they will implement this plan twice. Once in Egypt and once in Gerar. Both times, when Sarah is kidnapped, the royal households are afflicted with illness because G-d is protecting Sarah.

Questions

1. A simple reading of this story is problematic since Abraham's concern that required them not to disclose their true relationship, assumes that G-d would not protect Abraham from getting killed. Did they doubt the importance of their mission and that is why they feared the power of mortal kings to destroy them? Could it be possible that Abraham and Sarah were not aware of the importance of their work? A simple reading of the text leads us to this improbable conclusion.

2. Having had Sarah already taken into the Egyptian harem, why wasn't Abraham extra careful to protect Sarah when they went to Gerar? He is asked by the King of Gerar why he was initially suspicious of Gerar. Abraham responds that they seem godless <and are therefore dangerous>.

"I realized that this place is missing the fear of G-d" (*Genesis* 20:11).

The chapter begins by telling us that Abraham "often visited Gerar." (20:1) so we know he was fully aware of Gerar's godlessness. Why does he put Sarah in jeopardy by bringing her to a godless place? Especially because she had been previously taken by the Egyptian harem under a similar pretext.

3. Why doesn't Abraham consider the danger to Sarah if their plan unravels? Should their true relationship be discovered, Sarah would be trapped in a Harem unable to escape and her life would then be in danger from an angry King who would be angered by the deception.

Answer

Being aware that Abraham's objective was to bring monotheism to the world allows us to reread these stories with discernible eyes.

We must conclude that their trust in G-d meant they were unafraid of the danger posed by the deception. Because these stories were included in the Bible confirms that they are examples of Abraham and Sarah's efforts to bring monotheism to the world. They must have seen this policy of kidnapping trophy wives, for the royal courts, as an opportunity to convert the harems to monotheism.

The text validates this approach in the unusual way the story begins. Abraham tells Sarah, "I realize you are a good-looking woman"(*Genesis* 12:11). It is unlikely that the Bible notes that Abraham is suddenly telling his wife, she is attractive. The emphasis of this opening statement could have been that Abraham tells Sari to be alert since they are entering a dangerous environment. Instead, we are told that Abraham is assessing Sarah's beauty, for the likelihood of being kidnapped. It must mean there is an underlying and distinct theme in the conversation that needs to be heard. Like all the stories of Abraham, we are given the strategies of Abraham and Sarah to convert the world to monotheism. He is actually saying," Let's use your beauty to achieve our objective."

Sarah was willing to go along with the plan because once she had access to the royal harem, she could thereby influence the Elites via the royal household. Rashi (*Genesis* 12:5) tells us that Sarah had already developed the ability to influence women when she was in Haran. The Torah records two separate times that they tried to influence Kings in this fashion. First with an Egyptian King and afterward with Abimelech, King of Gerar. Sarah was already close to ninety years old at the second attempt. Clearly, collecting women for the royal harem was for reasons other than satisfying the carnal lusts or birthing an heir for the royals. In ancient times, the harem was a method for a King to make alliances with other regimes by marrying the relatives of foreign kings. It was also prestigious for a royal to maintain a collection of trophy wives. This effort to expand their harems gives us a clue as to the real purpose of why Abraham and Sarah tried to gain access to the harems.

The Egyptian Pharaoh said it straight out "Why did you say that she was your sister? So, I should take her to myself as a wife?" (ibid.12:19) Pharaoh knew the effort was deliberate. Scripture is expecting the reader like Pharaoh to discern the couple's true objective.

In both instances, they were found out before they could succeed.[8] After failing to convert the elites, Abraham tried to spread monotheism by preaching to the commoners (see chapter 9). Unfortunately, in all four examples provided by Scripture, Abraham cannot convince either the royals or the common people of Canaan to adopt monotheism. It is important to emphasize that Sarah stood next to him and shared his vision. The plan to infiltrate the Egyptian Pharaoh's harem was done only after Sarah consented to be abducted by the king's minions. It was Sarah, who was determined to bring monotheism to the world even at the cost of personal peril. Sarah was prepared to spread monotheism among the harem elites.

Another validation for approaching the kidnappings as examples of Sarah's determination to bring monotheism to the world is the fact that the Bible provides only a few stories that pertain to Sarah, yet we know she was recognized as beloved by the Lord. Along with Abraham, G-d changed her name to show that the covenant of the BBH is with both of them.

Sarah Continued: The Visitors at Mamre (Genesis 18)

Biblical Background

Once Abraham completes the Brit Milah by circumcising all the males in his entire camp, he is visited by angels at Mamre. He invites the angels to dine and quickly assembles a meal. He asks several members of his household to supply provisions for the meal and we are indirectly told the menu of meat, bread, and yogurt. The angels sit down to dine with him and advise him that he should expect the birth of Isaak from Sarah. They also share with him the imminent destruction of Sodom. Sarah upon hearing of her impending pregnancy has her personal inner thoughts recorded by scripture. She seemingly marvels at the news of expected pregnancy just as Abraham marveled at the same news in the previous chapter at the Brit Milah. Abraham is given the angel's angry response to Sarah's thoughts. They accuse Sarah of doubting G-d's ability to enable her to bear Abraham's child. Even while being assured of his greatest wish, the gift of having a worthy heir, Abraham instead turns to another issue raised by the angels. When informed of the fate of Sodom, he tries to save them by appealing to G-d's innate qualities of fairness and justice.

Questions

1. Sarah has become a tragic figure, she fights with her handmaid, Hagar (*Genesis* 16:6), she argues with her husband (ibid.16:5) and now she seemingly even mocks the Lord. What has become of this remarkable woman who, like Abraham was born a polytheist, converted to monotheism, and has suffered untold embarrassment by remaining barren?

2. When the angel asks Abraham, "Why did Sarah mock the prophecy that she will bear a child." The accusation was not true. In fact, the Bible tells us exactly what Sarah's inner thoughts were. She marvels at giving

birth at ninety years old, just as Abraham did at the Bris Milah and Sarah is also concerned that she and her elderly husband will now be raising a child. When confronted by the angel's accusation of her having mocked; the Bible says she was afraid and therefore defended herself and said she did not mock the prophesy. What was she afraid of, her inner thoughts cannot be punishable regardless of their content? In addition, who was Sarah afraid of? Abraham was not a violent husband.

3. Although she was asked to prepare bread for the meal with the visitors, her bread was not listed as one of the foods that were displayed to the guests. What happened to Sarah's bread?

Answers

It is incumbent upon us all to understand the greatness of Sarah. She is included in the Brit Milah both by the promise of a child and the changing her name from Sari to Sarah. Our mother Sarah was pure in action and thought. We will delve deep into the text to understand her. The hidden story of Sarah requires that we:

1. First, confirm that there is a hidden story behind the story. Then, reread the text using our knowledge of Sumerian culture, as we seek to uncover Sarah's hidden story.

2. Finally, reinterpret the life of Sarah and salute her contribution to the dissemination of monotheism.

Understanding the Text

Rabbinic commentator, Rashi, is encouraged by reading the text to see a hidden second story describing the visitors at Mamre. Rashi points out that there are dots above the word "to him" in the sentence "the angels said to him"(*Genesis* 18:9). Which means we must read the sentence as having a double meaning. This conversation that the angels are having with Abraham in Mamre which can so easily be understood by the casual reader actually has another story being played out in the background.

An in-depth reading of the text leaves us perplexed. We read in the Bible's previous chapter that one detail of the Brit Milah is that Sarah will have a child in a year. Therefore, Sarah was well aware of the promise of a child from the details of the Brit Milah. Having a child is not new information to her, so we cannot accept a simple reading of the text that Sarah heard the news and mocked it. Something more must be happening here. When Rashi reads this chapter, he comments that there are two threads that must be followed.

Rashi, gives his first analysis of the hidden entendre in the chapter with the repetition of the word "Vayayra" (ibid.18:2). He explains the first "Vayayra" means "and he saw." In contrast, the second one means "and he understood." What did Abraham suddenly understand?

Rashi analyzes a second indication that there is a hidden message in the simple story. As mentioned above, the dots on top of the word "to him" in ibid.18:9. Rashi interprets the simple reading as "they said to him"; because of the dots there must be an alternative reading of the word "to him." What were the angels really saying to Abraham?

We have shown the two indicators that Rashi found in the Biblical text which begs the reader to uncover a second story. This second story gives us an insight into Sarah's thinking and commitment to monotheism. It will allow us to discover the greatness of our mother Sarah.

Contribution from Sumerian Archeology: Rereading the Text

Thanks to our knowledge of Sumerian culture, we are aware that, according to Sumerian legal tradition, a meal was required to complete a treaty. This will be a key to discovering the elusive second story hidden behind the visitors at Mamre.

The treaty requirement for a concluding fete would explain why Abraham is intent on sharing a meal with the angels. Both he and Sarah understand the angels have come to eat the meal which will conclude the Brit Milah. Abraham asks his aide to prepare the meats, and he asks Sarah to prepare the bread. We learn from the menu of meat and bread that they are the basic requirements for the treaty's concluding meal.

We know Sarah did not prepare the bread that Abraham asked her to prepare. Scripture enumerates the foods that were set in front of the angels and the bread is missing.[9]

By not preparing the bread, Sarah is intentionally sabotaging the meal which is to conclude the Brit Milah. Sarah does not want the Brit Milah enacted.

The two versions of the story intertwine to give us a complementary picture of Sarah. The first version is the simple reading of the text where Sarah is in her tent unable to make the cakes. Rabbinical sources claim that was because she resumed her monthly cycles and did not want to contaminate the bread accidentally. The hidden second version is about the damage she caused to concluding the Brit Milah and that is what the angels are addressing when they ask Abraham about Sarah.[10] With a possible threat to her promised child from the disinherited Ishmael, we now understand why Sarah cannot admit to blocking the Brit Milah.[11]

By blocking the Brit Milah, Sarah has stopped the blessings that were enumerated for Ishmael.[12] When the angels point out that the covenant has failed because Sarah has done something to prevent its enactment. Sarah is scared of Hagar and Ishmael for preventing Ishmael from getting the blessings in the Brit Milah. Sarah shows that she does not care about the personal embarrassment she suffers for undermining the Brit Milah. Sarah is steadfast in her belief that Ishmael will not inherit any of the blessings given to Abraham.

In an attempt to have Sarah reveal her true intentions, the angels intentionally question her level of faith. Intentionally, they misconstrued her response to their announcement. They wrongly accuse Sarah of not trusting that the Lord will give her a child although she is old. They must feel confident that upon hearing this accusation, Sarah will reconsider and allow the Brit Milah to conclude. They are wrong, Sarah is willing to be insulted and accused of doubting the Lord if that results in Ishmael not inheriting any of Abraham's blessings. Once again, we see Sarah's remarkable resolve to stand against pagans and paganism.[13]

Sarah's Pathos

Sarah is convinced that she successfully torpedoed the Bris Milah. The tent of Abraham is operating under the objective of the Bris Bain Habasorim and therefore continues under the original objective, which was for Abraham and Sarah to help bring about a universal conversion to monotheism. The naming of Isaak allows us to see this clearly. We know Sarah is continuing to work under the BBH when Abraham names Isaak because she focuses on how people outside the Abrahamic tent will respond,

"All who hear about it will laugh for me." (ibid.21:6). Sarah is focused on the pagan world's response instead of focusing on how the child affects herself and Abraham. In contrast, we find that when the tribes of Jacob are named, they are given names to reflect a personal bond between parent and child. Their names do not reflect the parent's expectations of what the child's birth will have on the outside world. Sarah seems to be an exception; she attributes Abraham naming her child Isaak to how other people hearing of her late age birth will respond.

This confusion about the purpose for naming her child Isaak tells us that when he is named by Abraham, Sarah continues to see her life as part of the universal mission to bring monotheism to the world. She does not recognize that the mission was contracted to a parochial effort, just the family of Abraham. To Sarah, Brit Milah was a commandment but not a mission changer because due to her efforts, it never became operational.

Another hint that Sarah thought the Brit Milah was not operational, can be inferred from scripture. Although Abraham circumcised Isaak on the eighth day, as far as the text relates, a party wasn't organized. However, a party was made when Isaak was weaned. Abraham and Sarah see the birth of Isaak as an opportunity to exhibit to the outside world the miracle of prayer in a monotheistic context.

Once the covenant is completed, at the Binding of Isaak, all the inducements to leave Haran have now been transferred into specific blessings. This is when Sarah becomes painfully aware that she was unable to stop the blessings of the Brit Milah going to Ishmael,

"I will bless him, and make him fruitful, increasing his numbers very greatly. He will father twelve princes, and I will make him into a great nation (*Genesis* 17:20)

We are given a hint of Sarah's dramatic, determined efforts to exclude Ishmael and retrieve the blessing for Isaak. The Bible lists and details a portion of the fulfillment of Ishmael's blessings that he and his descendants had received.

"These were Ishmael's sons, and these names were given to their towns and encampments. There were twelve princes for their nations."(*Genesis* 25:16) This fulfillment of the blessing he received at the Brit Milah, is ironically mentioned in the same chapter that Sarah dies. Sarah's failed efforts to block Ishmael from receiving the blessings are thus forever linked to her chapter in the Bible. If only Sarah was able to retrieve the blessing "and I will make him into a great nation"(*Genesis* 17:20) the Arab Conquest and the rise of Islam could never have happened.

It is perhaps a lesson to her children. Regardless of our intense feelings or passion to achieve an outcome, no matter how holy the cause, we cannot control the universal divine plan. Sarah's intense commitment to monotheism did not guarantee her success in her efforts to block Ishmael, she lost that battle. However, when we look at her children, four thousand years later, we can safely say she won the war. Polytheism is on the scrap heap of history, while monotheism is normative.

Immediately after the completion of the Brit, at the binding of Isaak, we read of her passing. Sarah waited until she was ninety to bear a child and she passed away without ever seeing her grandchildren or even the marriage of Isaak. Her golden life of dedication to monotheism ends sadly. We often remember her only as an ardent supporter of Abraham without fully understanding her constant support of monotheism or her personal pain. May G-d grant us the wisdom to comprehend the virtues and pathos of our mother Sarah who, befittingly, has the lofty title of the mother of the Jewish people.

Chapter Eight:

Suzerain-Vassal Treaty

This chapter is devoted to a review of the S/V treaty hidden in the Torah It uses "BBH" as a shorthand for the Brit Bain Habasorim

Now that we combined the BBH, Brit Milah, and the Binding of Isaak into one large document. How does it all come together?

At the BBH:

The document's primary objective: Transfer the land of Canaan to Abraham and his offspring. In exchange Abraham and his children are to continue to have a belief in monotheism with a practical result that an adherent maintains a belief in positive outcomes (*Genesis*15:6) and all males are circumcised when they are eight days old (*Genesis*17:10).[14] It begins with the standard format, as follows:

The legal and technical format of the Suzerain / Vassal Treaty:

S/V treaty: Introduction: Naming the Suzerain and his previous interactions with the Vassal.

As per the S/V agreement: And He said to him, "I am the Lord, who brought you forth from Ur of the Chaldees, to give you this land to inherit it."(*Genesis* 15:7)

Next section in the s/v agreement: What the vassal can expect from the Suzerain and what the Vassal is required to do in return:

Abraham is promised: To you and your offspring I will give the land where you are now living as a foreigner, (*Genesis* 17:8). The purpose of the covenant is the transferring of the land to Abraham. In return, he is required to perform the fulfilment of the law "You must circumcise every male" (*Genesis* 17:10) and possibly other statutes.

Next section in the s/v treaty: What happens if the Vassal fails to perform: And the birds of prey descended upon the carcasses, and Abram drove them away.(*Genesis* 15:11) failure to support the Suzerain will be met by dire consequences as exemplified by being attacked by birds of prey.

Next section in the s/v treaty: Both Suzerain and Vassal walk through the space created by the cut animals. As they walk through the Vassal is required to daub blood on the ends of each cut carcass delineating the pathway.

"and behold, a smoking furnace and a fire brand, which passed between these parts."(*Genesis* 15:17).

Abraham does not walk between the parts.

וַיֹּאמֶר בִּי נִשְׁבַּעְתִּי (*Genesis* 22:16) G-d says, I alone swore.

Next section in the s/v treaty: The Vassal adopts a new name to reflect his new status.

וְלֹא־יִקָּרֵא עוֹד אֶת־שִׁמְךָ אַבְרָם וְהָיָה שִׁמְךָ אַבְרָהָם כִּי אַב־הֲמוֹן גּוֹיִם (*Genesis* 17:5)Abram will now be called Abraham.

Sari your wife — do not call her by the name Sari, for Sarah is her name. (*Genesis* 17:15)

The next and final section is a shared meal which finalizes the deal. The Bible is clear that the BBH is the legal basis for the land transfer (*Genesis* 15:18). On the day of the BBH, Abraham is told, "To your seed, I have given this land."

The Bible's next story seems to be out of place to be included in the legal transfer of Canaan. The story of Hagar seems to appear in the middle of the Israelite legal contract. We must therefore conclude it is there to provide us with a definition of the term "Banei Ubancha",(*Genesis* 16:5) which will be used later on. At the Brit Milah, the Lord uses this term to describe Abraham's new more limited mission. Therefore one reason we need this story is to define Brit Milah's legal terminology.[15]

At Brit Milah: Changes are made.

Abraham is introduced as:

וַיְהִי אַבְרָם בֶּן־תִּשְׁעִים שָׁנָה וְתֵשַׁע שָׁנִים וַיֵּרָא ה' אֶל־אַבְרָם ויאמר אליו אני ה' התהלך לפני והיה תמים

Land transfers require that both parties need to be identified-Identifying the buyer as well as the identity of the seller. We read at the BBH that G-d is identified as "He who brought you forth from Ur." Here, Abraham is identified as a "Tamim."No longer is the Torah referencing a blessing that the whole world will be blessed or influenced through Abraham, there has been a change in emphasis from the BBH's universal mission to a new perspective. In this new perspective just Abraham's personal circle (banei ou baincha) is to be monotheist. Abraham is not going along with this retrenchment. He expresses this by doubting to father children at his age.

Abraham projects his failures to convince Canaanites of monotheism onto G-d's new mission for Abraham by saying I and my wife are too old to have children. This sudden expression of doubt is telling. When Abraham projects his own failures on G-d's plan for Abraham's zera? It reveals that Abraham is suffering sadness for failing to affect the Canaanite polytheistic mentality. This sadness is causing him to doubt the ability for things to improve. He can't see success even with this new mission.

In Sumerian culture, it was usual to first craft an agreement and then test it out. If successful it is followed by the final treaty. Here the test-out did not go well and the treaty reflects a modification. There will be a smaller scope (Banei ou Baincha) made just between G-d and Abraham without universal overtones. In addition, the grand gesture of giving Abraham the land of Canaan as a gift is modified to now require the observance of laws to be worthy of staying in the land.

Binding of Isaak

G-d uses kind terms to have Abraham accept the trial which is designed to aid Abraham out of his sadness. Abraham aces the test and now Abraham receives additional blessings. He is promised that his children will be a blessing to all nations on the earth. Ironically, now that the Brit has become a personal covenant, Abraham's dream of universal impact becomes assured.

In addition, the land of Canaan will have cities built and waiting for them.

According to Sumerian culture, the additional blessings given to Abraham after the Binding of Isaak match the tradition of the accuser giving a reward to the subject if the subject wins the trial. The upgrade of the blessings would reflect that. Although the treaty is already completed the upgrades are just an addition to the earlier blessings and do not affect the treaty's original provisions.

Chapter Nine:

Wells: Welcome to Canaan

Biblical Background

Abraham was seventy-five when he left Haran. He takes his nephew, Lot, with him. Abraham immediately travels throughout the land of Canaan. Due to a famine, he moves to Egypt, where Sarah is kidnapped and released with Abraham receiving great wealth from Pharaoh. Abraham returned to Canaan and settled in Hebron. His nephew, Lot, is captured by a gang of kings who take him and all of Sodom captive. They are all saved when Abraham executes a successful night raid. Abraham then petitions G-d for a legal transfer of Canaan to himself and his children. The Pact between the Halves is performed, Abraham is given Hagar as a baby-making wife and Ishmael is born. Abraham is given the requirement of circumcision.

Abraham was ninety-nine years old when he and Ishmael were circumcised. Visitors come to Abraham and notify him of the upcoming birth of Isaak and the destruction of Sodom. Lot is saved while the rest of Sodom is destroyed. Sarah is kidnapped by Abimelech and released.

Abraham was one hundred years old when Isaak was born and circumcised. Hagar and Ishmael are expelled from Abraham's household. Abimelech agrees to a treaty regarding Abraham's well at Baer Sheva and attempts to make a peace treaty with Abraham. Abraham is tested with the binding of Isaak.

Questions

1. Why does the Bible pair the story of Hagar being expelled from Abraham's home with the story of Baer Sheva, a peace treaty attempted with Abimelech of Gerar?

2. Abraham makes a peace treaty with Abimelach (*Genesis*:32) that is supposed to last generations and yet we find another peace treaty with Abimelach (*Genesis* 26:30) and Isaac, just one generation later. Why the second treaty?

3. In *Genesis* (26:15) we read that Isaak opened wells that his father dug and the Philistines had closed up We didn't see any mention of Abraham digging wells in the Biblical stories about Abraham.

Answer

In Sumer the enemy was clear. Abraham saw the Temples Priests and Elites as dominating and controlling a mass of superstitious commoners. Canaan was very different, the effort to teach monotheism was going to need a different approach. The population was divided into clans living in small rural communities. In Sumer, the land was irrigated by the city's well-developed canal network. The canals fed into a network of sluices and troughs that fed the land and the livestock. In Canaan, the only water source was the well. Abraham assessed that if his message of monotheism was to spread it would happen at the wells.

Digging a well 100 feet down to the underground aquifer was a great effort, but once built it would attract people needing to re-hydrate their flocks. While they were at the well, Abraham provided both food and lodging (see Rashi, Eshel *Genesis* 21:33). When the shepherds visited the well Abraham gave them food. He asked them to bless the one<LORD> whose food they have eaten. Unfortunately, this strategy did not go well and soon the wells were abandoned. As I mentioned in the introduction, the Torah is careful to avoid recording Abraham's failures and therefore we do not hear about them until Isaak reopens them (successfully?).

However, we do have one example of Abraham digging wells, it is when Abraham opens a well on the property of Abimelech, king of Gerar. The idolaters resented it and argued with him. Eventually, Abraham tries to smooth things over with Abimelech and he is able to resolve the well issue by buying it straight out. When Abimelech tries to build on this new relationship, he asks Abraham to cut a multi-generational peace treaty with him. As we have previously mentioned, cutting a treaty requires that both parties sit down to a joint meal with foods supplied by both sides. Without a concluding feast, the treaty is canceled. For unknown reasons both Abimelech and his general take leave from Abraham before this crucial meal that would have concluded the deal (*Genesis* 21:32). This resulted in Isaak negotiating another deal. At Isaak's treaty, Abimelech and his general stay for the meal, and the covenant is enacted (*Genesis* 26:30).

After the Brit Melah Abraham is facing failure on multiple fronts. This includes his failure to convert members in his household, Hagar and Ishmael, to monotheism. This story is paired with another example of his failings. This one, as stated above (p. 27) is in the diplomatic arena i.e. Abimelech of Gerar.

Lastly, Abraham was deeply concerned with the fate of the Sodomites and tried to negotiate a life raft for them. Here too Abraham was unable to save them. Maybe it was this combination of factors that led Abraham to begin to doubt himself and which then led to the next chapter, The Binding of Isaak, which begins with the words "It was after these things that G-d appeared to test Abraham" (ibid. 22:1).

Teacher's Notes for Chapter 9

In Sumerian culture there was a hierarchical paradigm that separated the Elites from the commoners. As a Sumerian Abraham would have been sensitive to this division and when he moved to Canaan, he would view the social structure as requiring a different set of tactics from those he applied in Sumer. We find in Scripture that Abraham developed a two-pronged effort in his efforts to spread monotheism. Each story is another unique strategy. Since the Bible does not reference that Abraham was able to achieve any meaningful success in Canaan, we can reasonably say there wasn't any great success.

As proof of his only limited success, we find that when he musters an army to fight the four kings, according to Rashi he only had his servant Eliezer and assistants Anar, Eshkol & Mamre (*Genesis* 14:24). Another indication that Canaan was not receptive to monotheism might be that Abraham was insistent that Isaak's bride come from Haran and not the areas he was preaching to. Could this be because he felt the people in Canaan were hopelessly lost to polytheism? Without references indicating Abraham's success, we can deduce that there wasn't any.

The elites of Canaan consisted of the priestly class and the royal households. Abraham made two attempts to try to influence them. Both times Sarah was his willing accomplice. The harems of Mesopotamia were used not only used as secure homes for the king's wives but were also used as a place to collect women that were useful for political purposes i.e. treatise with other kings to secure peace or expand borders and to display to the populace as trophies. Surely it was this latter purpose that the Bible is referring to when Abraham turns to Sarah and says "Now, I know you are beautiful women" Clearly, he is telling his ninety-year-old wife that she would be desirable to a king looking to add a trophy to his Harem. Her grace and elegance would make her desirable to the Egyptian king causing the king to kill Abraham so he could add Sarah to his harem.

From Abraham's perspective, this was an opportunity to influence the Elites from within the palace walls. When Sarah was abducted, she maintained the lie that she was not Abraham's wife but his sister. At the same time, she would disseminate monotheism to the Harem and eventually the King himself. The All Mighty immediately punishes Pharaoh for his rash behavior. Instead of taking responsibility for his behavior, he blames Abraham for plotting to undermine him. Abraham does not achieve his primary objective but leaves Egypt a very wealthy man. The question arises as to why G-d doesn't let the plan play out but aborts it by bringing a plague to Pharaoh's palace. Pharaoh connects the plagues to the abduction of Sarah abduction and concludes he was deceived. After bestowing great wealth on Abraham Pharaoh ejects both Sarah and Abraham from Egypt.

We can only speculate as to why G-d was willing to abort Abraham's plan by plaguing Pharoah's household. Was Sarah's dignity remaining intact more important than their mission? Does G-d respond to evil irrespective of the greater good? There is certainly room for a homily on this topic.

Taking a loss doesn't prevent Abraham from trying again. This time he chooses a small seaside kingdom, near present-day, Gaza. Once again, the king, Abimelech King of Gerar, abducts Sarah for his Harem. However, he gets a revelation in a dream that directs him to return Sarah and advises him to ask Abraham to pray for him. Shockingly, while he seems oblivious to the possibility that there are serious consequences for kidnapping, he qualifies to receive a prophecy. Abimelach stands in contrast to Pharaoh he wants to understand what went wrong and doesn't seek to lay blame on others.

Chapter Ten:

Hagar & Ishmael (Competition Challenges Everyone)

Biblical Background

Hagar is brought to Abram by Sari to act as a baby-making concubine. When she conceives, Sari accuses Hagar of demeaning her mistress and afflicts her causing her to run away. An angel lures her back by promising her blessings for her son who is destined to be born and even tells her to name the child Ishmael. She pronounces that she has been visited by the god of seeing. Indeed, a son is born and Abraham names him Ishmael (*Genesis* 16). At the Brit Milah, in addition to promising Abraham the land of Canaan, G-d bestows additional blessings on Ishmael (ibid 17:20) Sarah sees that Ishmael is worshipping idols and insists that Ishmael will not inherit with Isaak.(ibid.21:10) Abraham consults with God and as per Sarah's demand, Hagar and Ishmael are evicted. When Hagar and Ishmael are evicted from Abraham's household, Ishmael is not feeling well. Then they run out of water. Hagar leaves Ishmael under the shade of bushes and then moves away from him because she says she doesn't want to witness the child's death. After being expelled from Abraham's household, and she can no longer care for her sickly child she separates herself from Ishmael and begins to cry. Hagar is told "not to fear", which to a pagan means to stop praying, because the boy's prayers have already been heard.

Questions

1. There seem to be two missing sentences in the Bible: Where are they?

- When Abraham names his son Ishmael (*Genesis* 16:15) that is the name, the angel tells Hagar to name him (*Genesis* 16:12) and yet we don't find that Hagar actually tells this to Abraham

- At the Brit Milah, Abraham is offered the land of Canaan with additional blessings. In addition, he is advised of the birth of Isaak. Unexpectedly, we read "And regarding Ishmael, I have heard you" and yet we don't find that Abraham asked about Ishmael receiving blessings.

2. As a human mother, how could Hagar lack the compassion to stay with Ishmael? She should not let him die alone.

3. At the Brit Milah Hagar receives blessings for Ishmael even before Isaak is conceived. Why is Ishmael in the Brit Milah?

Answer

Hagar was a product of her times. As an Egyptian living in Canaan, she was polytheistic. But as a member of Abraham's household, she was comfortable with visits from Angels. Yet she refused to become a monotheist. This was why Sari hates Hagar causing her to run away before Ishmael's birth. The Torah also despises the idol worshipers, and that answers our first question, as to why sentences that were spoken by pagans are deleted, especially when they can be deduced from the text. With this understanding, we can say that the missing sentences were purposely omitted because they would have been spoken by Hagar, an avowed pagan.

To answer our second question, we will look at Hagar's world view. She was taught by the temple priests that if one did not serve the gods in the exact correct way there would be dire consequences. Coincidentally the temple priests claimed that they were the only ones who knew the correct method to serve the gods. After Ishmael is caught by Sarah worshiping idols, Hagar and Ishmael become homeless, and Ishmael falls ill, then they have no water and no hope. Hagar thinks that Ishmael must have angered the gods by not serving the idols correctly. Being a Polytheist, she cannot envision positive outcomes and immediately loses hope and tries to separate herself from her son's doom even if that requires that he dies alone.

To answer the final question, we will first see how Hagar and her story have become woven around and into our Brit Milah we will then explain why her story is imperative to the Brit Milah.

    A. Pre-Brit Milah:

When Hagar receives the blessings, she responds by calling her angel "the god of seeing." In Sumeria, each god was assigned its own unique domain. There was a separate god for the land, the sea, the harvest, etc., By calling her god "the seeing god", she restricts her god to the domain of seeing thereby she reveals herself to be an idol worshiper. This contrasts with Abraham who also names his G-d after he was stopped from human sacrifice at the binding of Isaac. He names his God "the God that will be seen" <by his actions> which would be appropriate for a monotheist to assign descriptions but not domains.

B. At the Brit Milah and post Brit Milah:

Ishmael gets the promise that he will be fruitful (*Genesis* 17:20). This is not a unique blessing; it is the same blessing given to Noah. Ishmael receives a second blessing (*Genesis* 17:20) at the Brit Milah that he will beget twelve princes. Rashi points out the term of "princes to their nation" as meaning "like a cloud" they were just like a cloud that would pass. When Ishmael dies (*Genesis* 25:16) at 137, scripture provides the names of the twelve princes; they made no long-term impact, and the world was not blessed through them.

However, Ishmael gets two long-term blessings 1) I will multiply him exceedingly and 2)I will make him into a great nation (*Genesis* 18:20). This blessing is repeated when Hagar is told after her eviction from Abraham's camp that "I shall make him into a great nation": (*Genesis* 21:18) This blessing was a primary blessing since it was one of the inducements to Abraham to leave Haran. We need to ask: Is giving Ishmael the blessing the fulfillment of the inducement? Does giving Ishmael this blessing mean it can no longer go to Isaac? We will show that Sarah certainly thought this blessing must be rescinded. She acted with the hope that she might be able to redirect this blessing to Isaak (see chapter 7).

We know it was Sarah's intention to prevent Ishmael from getting any of Abraham's blessings since when she had him kicked out of Abraham's tent for idol worshiping, she doesn't say because Ishmael might influence Isaac. Instead, she says I don't want Ishmael to inherit with Isaac. She seems to think that evicting Ishmael will cause, his inheritance, the blessing "I will make you into a great nation" will then go to Isaak. However, Sarah cannot retrieve this blessing. Even after the eviction, Hagar is assured that Ishmael will receive the blessing of I shall make him into a great nation (ibid. 21:18).

We must accept that Isaak does not get the blessing of becoming a great nation, Empire, and Colonialism, will never be a Jewish trait. When the modern state of Israel is accused of trying to exploit its neighbors via the European method of imperialism it is absurd factually, biblically and historically.

Although we have explained what Hagar gets from the Brit Milah, we have not yet explained why we need her and her polytheistic mindset to be part of Brit Milah.

To begin, we will first need to compare the many instances where we can compare Abraham's experiences to Hagar's experiences. Once we have found the similarities we can then discuss the differences. Here are some of the similarities.

- Both are suffering anxiety when they are addressed by the Lord.

- Abraham is dealing with a fear (see above Abraham-Sodom) that G-d is responding with "Fear not Abraham, I am your shield."

- Hagar is scared of Sari probably because of the Sumerian law that a mistress can have a handmaiden beaten because of insurrection.

- Both are given instructions.

- Abraham is told to take animals for the BBH.

- Hagar is told to return to Sari 3. Both are told by G-d what name to give their child

- Abraham is told twice to expect a child but is given his name, Isaak, once (*Genesis* 17:19)

- Hagar is told what to name her child at the same time she is given blessings to the child (*Genesis* 16:11)

- Both are given a glimpse into the future path their children will experience that is first bleak then hopeful

- Abraham is told his children will inherit the land after first suffering enslavement.

- Hagar is told her son will die peacefully after first being despised for being a bandit.

5. Both have their child who received the promises of fruitfulness face peril and yet they say nothing to protest G-d's seemingly going back on his word:

- Abraham is given the Binding of Isaak

- Hagar leaves Ishmael to die when they are evicted from Abraham's camp, and they run out of water.

6. Both are told that he/she will be exceedingly fruitful

- Abraham is shown the stars at the Brit Melah when he is assured of fruitfulness.

- Hagar was told at her first vision (*Genesis* 16:10). Here she is assured blessing that she will be exceedingly fruitful.

These points with the corresponding counterpoints are key to providing an answer to Why we need to talk about Hagar at this point of the Brit Milah. She is given the same opportunities as Abraham to see G-D's hidden hand in the world, yet she lacks the mindful awareness that monotheism requires and remains an idolatress. However, the Torah gives us dramatic events so we can see the difference in Abraham's reaction compared to Hagar's reaction These events will allow us to define the term, Monotheism and how being a monotheist has a practical impact on our lives.

The Torah shows us two examples where Abraham & Hagar diverge. These examples will reveal how a monotheist interfaces with the world as compared to a polytheist. Hagar will act as a foil to better understand Abraham's monotheism. These examples are as follows:

A belief in positive outcomes

The primary difference between the monotheist, Abraham and the polytheist, Hagar. Is the belief in positive outcomes. At the Binding of Isaak, Abraham is confident Isaak will be saved and tells his assistants that both he and Isaak will return from Mt.Moriah (*Genesis* 22:5). In contrast, Hagar, ever the idolatress, moves away from her sick son expecting him to die. "Let me not see the child's death" (*Genesis* 21:16). Even a one-time loving mother, when traumatized by life's vicissitudes, can turn from a nurturer to a selfish wrench. Instead of standing by her ailing son to give him comfort, she stays far away unable to envision positive endings for Ishmael. Instead, she selfishly cries and protects herself from the pain of seeing her child pass away. She is not irrational, based on her polytheistic upbringing she responds to Ishmael's condition from that viewpoint. Ishmael was worshiping the gods when he was caught by Sarah. Since then he has become homeless, fell seriously ill, and is now facing hunger and thirst. Hagar doesn't see this as a failure of idolatry instead she feels the situation is hopeless because Ishmael didn't serve the gods correctly and that is why he is doomed. She is so convinced of his doom she doesn't even ask her "god of seeing" who bestowed blessings on Ishmael to prevent his passing away prior to the fulfillment of the blessings. She was taught that when the gods are not served correctly there are dire consequences for the practitioners. In her mindset, Ishmael is doomed because he failed to serve the gods correctly and there is no chance of salvation. The Torah gives us this insight into polytheistic mentality to allow us to understand how monotheism stands in opposition to Hagar's views.

A willingness to take positive actions to achieve desired   outcomes.

When the text writes "G-d opened her eyes, and she beheld a well of water" we are informed that G-d needed to open her eyes for Hagar to see the water. Hagar was trained by her pagan priest that humanity was incapable of saving itself from divine wrath. Without divine intervention, Hagar refuses to even search for the well. Her preconceived notions of humanity being subject to a pagan god that needed to be constantly appeased has resulted in a complete refusal to pursue viable options. Only when the angel intervenes to open her eyes to the well can she then see it. The pagan priests told their adherents that any deviation from their instruction would bring dire retribution from the gods. She was so convinced of the pagan priest's narrative, that she could not even see a solution lying before her. Abraham, in contrast, takes the initiative and raises his own eyes, without the need for G-d to open his eyes he sees a solution to his problem. He wants to bring a sacrifice, yet he did not bring along an animal for a burnt offering. When faced with a spiritual problem he is confident that he can take decisive actions that will result in positive outcomes. Again, the Torah is giving us another important insight into the difference in behaviors between a polytheist and a monotheist. Hagar's inability or refusal to see the reality that the water was in front of her confirms that, like her son, Hagar continued to be an idolatress even as a member of Abraham's household. Abraham, in contrast, does not need an angel to open his eyes he "lifts up his eyes" and searches for a practical solution. Abraham's monotheist religion empowers him to achieve positive outcomes while polytheism demeans the practitioner to the point of impotency.

Now all has been revealed. Now we know why we need to have Hagar displayed in the Brit Milah. In every covenant, there is a bringing together of two parties. Each party must bring something to the table. At Brit Milah, we are not told what Abraham brings to the table. Many casual readers make the mistake of thinking that in exchange for performing a circumcision, the Jews receive Canaan. In fact, circumcision is just a sign of the Covenant but agreeing to show a sign that there is a covenant does not qualify as an asset that Abraham can initially bring to the table. We only know that G-d, after agreeing to the transfer of Canaan to Abraham and his seed, then requires the sign of circumcision (*Genesis* 17:10). It is important to emphasize that being able to fulfill a condition of the covenant does not qualify the receiving party as a party to the covenant. Abraham still needs to have something to offer so he can enter into the covenant, but what does Abraham bring to the table?

He brings a belief in monotheism and a willingness to instruct others!

The Bible includes Hagar in the chapters that created the treaty to contrast the polytheistic Hagar to the monotheistic Abraham. Only by contrasting with Hagar do we see the asset, monotheism, that Abraham brings to the table. We manifest our monotheistic belief by trusting in positive outcomes and the wisdom that the world was created for humans to reach their maximum potential. In a polytheistic world, Abraham's wisdom was a sufficient asset that G-d was prepared to make an eternal covenant with him.

Only by contrasting Abraham to Hagar do we see Abraham's assets. Like Abraham, Hagar met with angels, who gave her blessings and direction and yet she was unable to embrace monotheism. Her polytheistic eyes saw shattered dreams, fears, and an inability to perceive G-d's invisible hand. Abraham saw the world through the eyes of a monotheist. He believed in positive outcomes and trusted that the world was made for humanity to take actions that would enable each person to reach their full potential. Abraham was determined to bring a sacrifice to thank G-d for helping him overcome great personal suffering, so he acted and behold the answer was waiting for him in the thicket. He was looking to take action and was assisted by G-d. This is exactly what the text means when it says "I will be to them for a G-d." When they take action, I will assist them with my righteous arm" (Isaiah 41:10). When the Jews came to live in Canaan, they had to fight wars to conquer it, but they had total confidence that G-d would ensure their success. So also today, the children of those mighty believers have again taken action and returned to the same Holy land promised to Abraham and assured via the Brit Bain Habasorim. May G-d, once again, ensure that their actions lead to personal and national success. Amen!

Both Abraham and Hagar were promised a child that would have varied blessings. Yet when that same child in in peril neither parent cries out and demands that the child's life must be saved because the child is blessed with special outcomes. Hagar is willing to live in a world where the gods are ruling and mankind is only here for the amusement of said gods. The gods are not held to any standard of responsibility that would require honesty- therefore a human cannot trust that the outcome of any of life's vicissitudes would be positive. Hagar accepts Ishmael's impending death as sad but inevitable and is therefore quiet and not demanding that the "god of seeing" keep his promise. Hagar does not believe in positive outcomes.

Abraham, in contrast, is living with the belief that the world was created for mankind to grow and flourish. Humans are not here to amuse or feed a desperately needy god. On the contrary, humankind relies on God to feed and clothe them. G-d's promise to Abraham that Isaak will be his seed that will receive the blessings bestowed on Abraham assures him that Isaak will not be sacrificed. Therefore, he is quiet when told to bring Isaak up as a sacrifice, Abraham is confident that Isaak is safe from harm. Furthermore, he tells the lads that "we will return" even while carrying the wood, flame & knife. Abraham is confident it will never happen. Abraham's G-d created humanity because he is leading them to a better future, therefore Abraham can believe in positive outcomes.

The Torah uses different terms to explain how the monotheist reacted to life compared to the polytheist. When Abraham lifted his eyes he saw a solution to a problem, but Hagar had to have her eyes opened by G-d, for her to see a solution. This then becomes our first pillar of monotheism. Now we will uncover the second pillar of monotheism which is that humankind has the power via actions and prayer to effect outcomes.

Again, we must compare the monotheist, Abraham to the pagan, Hagar, When Hagar refuses to see a solution for her dying child the angel must open her eyes (*Genesis* 21:19). Abraham in contrast opens his own eyes when looking for a solution (ibid. 22:13). He finds a solution and goes to take it. We can now understand that monotheism allows one to find and create solutions with the confidence that g-d intends for humanity to live meaningful lives. When Abraham lifted his eyes to look for a solution, he knew that he would find a sign of G-d's beneficence. A monotheist lives a life of personal growth and achievement, while a pagan is constantly trying to appease insatiable gods and sacrificing personal growth.

Chapter Eleven:

Leviticus 23:23-25 Explained

During the High Holy Days, we spend hours praying for a year of bounty and growth. We are never promised that our Rosh HaShana prayers will be heard. In fact, the Bible never uses the term, "Rosh Hashana" or talks about it being a day of judgment or a day of prayer. We first hear these terms in the Mishna. Other than referring to a remembrance of the shofar blowing, or a day of shofar blowing we are told little else of what this holiday is about (*Leviticus* 23:23-25). Our oral tradition tells us that the Bible is referring to a New Year's celebration. Only by looking at and contrasting it to Sumerian traditions can we see how the Torah was telling the Jews how the holiday was to be observed. As we have shown many laws and traditions in the Torah must be examined in their juxtapose-position to Sumerian culture at the time of Abraham.

1. The Sumerians celebrated the New Year in the month of the spring equinox.

Bible: In contrast, the Bible celebrates the New Year in the month of the autumn equinox

2. The celebration would continue for eleven days. During that time the different gods were taken out of the temples and paraded throughout the cities. There were even visits of gods to neighboring cities. (Daily Life in Ancient Mesopotamia, Karen Rhea Nemet-Nejat, Greenwood Press, Pg195)

Bible: The celebration lasts only ten days (the last day of Shmini Atzeret might be considered the eleventh day but is separated by the Sukkoth holiday).

The sacrifices brought at the Temple for Shmini Atzeret were similar to the sacrifices of the high holy days and differed from the sacrifices brought for the festivals. This hints that Shmini Atzeret is the eleventh day of the New Year celebration. The Rabbinic celebration of two days for Rosh Hashana is not stated in Scripture, however, its ancient origins might be a homage to the multiple-day celebration of the Sumerian/Mesopotamian New Year celebrations.

3. One of the highlights of the ceremonies was the slapping of the King by the temple priest. Especially good tidings were ascribed if the slap was hard enough to cause the king's eyes to well up in tears. In addition, there were fertility rituals involving

the king. The king in these rituals was viewed as representing humankind and his humiliation was intended to remind the people of Sumer of their inherent weakness and worthlessness.

The Bible's New Year celebration, in contrast, is not centered on celebrating G-d to the detriment of humankind but rather G-d welcomes mankind's prayers as they are being called to prayer with trumpets and the sound of the Shofar.

4. Another ritual of the Sumerian New Year celebration was reading sacred texts that told of the god's history and accomplishments. The constant theme was the uselessness of humankind and the loftiness of the gods and the elites.

Bible: in contrast celebrates Rosh Hashana by centering it around human beings and their future achievements. An ordinary person is encouraged to beseech from G-d good tidings for the upcoming year. Rosh Hashana looks to the future, and we celebrate it as a holiday because we trust that G-d will grant us a year of success and prosperity.

In the temple, the Shofar was accompanied by the silver trumpets that called the faithful to prayer (Rambam, Mishna Torah). Contemporary Biblical commentators refer to many things the sounds of the Shofar represent. Examples range from the cry of people seeking solace, to the royalty of the heavenly courts. This book is in search of origins. We therefore note that ultimately the Shofar helps the Jews to recognize that each individual's prayer is important to G-d, in contrast to the Sumerian culture where only the prayers of the elites were important.

Chapter Twelve:

Jewish Holidays: Some Unexpected Insights from Sumeria

New Years

All we are told about Rosh Hashana is that on the first day of the seventh month, we are to observe a "rest day" that is a "remembrance of the call of the Shofar." Rashi explains that the Torah is referring to Abraham finding the substitute for Isaac in the ram caught in the thicket. Given our expanded knowledge of Sumeria, we can provide an even more direct connection of Rosh Hashana to Abraham. We know that the context of the Bible is to stand in opposition to the pagan practices that Abraham saw in Sumer. As soon as the Bible states that there should be a holiday on the first of the month of the fall equinox the reader knows it is in contrast to the Sumerian New Year's celebration, held on the first day of the spring equinox. The reader is then told that it is a rest day. In ancient Sumer, only the high priest was given the power to declare a rest day. Telling people that they have a natural basic right to a rest day that does not require the declaration of the temple priests was radical and empowering.

The text then introduces the practice of trumpets to accompany the prayers of the congregants. This was equally radical since in Sumerian tradition there wasn't a method for the prayers of ordinary people to be heard by the gods. Only the priest had the power to communicate with the gods. Here the Bible is telling us the Jews are called to prayer with trumpets. This concept is not new since the Temple had silver trumpets that were blown to call the faithful to prayer (*Numbers* 10:10). So, we must logically conclude that this day of trumpets had a unique purpose that went beyond just summoning people to prayer. We can posit that the Torah is telling us that we are to dedicate a day of prayer on the very day we celebrate the New Year. Thus, we see that the text directed us to both pray for and celebrate the upcoming year.

Our tradition goes further; It elaborates on this opposition to paganism by redirecting the days emphasis. In ancient Sumer, the New Year celebration was only a celebration for the gods. The idols were taken out of the the temple and paraded through the streets. Occasionally there would be a visit from a god that was transferred from a neighboring city, A centerpiece of the celebration was a recitation of the "Epic of Creation," which told the people how the universe was created by the gods. These celebrations were intended to celebrate the god's and their past achievements. We are able to see how Rosh Hashana is an expression of that first monotheistic rule we derived above from comparing Hagar to Abraham. A human can trust in positive outcomes, we are not doomed to placate a never- satisfied deity. Our primary objective is to reach our human potential. It is not to prostrate ourselves to the elites. Ultimately, our Rosh Hashana prayers incorporates the belief that like Abraham at the Binding of Isaak, we believe that all events are a revelation of divine will and thereby must lead to positive outcomes. To reflect this belief, we celebrate the expected good in the year to come instead of focusing on giving thanks for the year that has passed. With great expectations we call Rosh Hashana a celebratory holiday and sing prayers with hope and praise. The belief in positive outcomes is also reflected in Our High Holy Days prayer books. These prayers incite the congregation to be more aware; in them, we honor our unique relationship with G-d, we celebrate the Shofar and recall the closeness with our Creator that prayer represents, and we remind ourselves of G'd's grace and the covenant he made with Abraham. In prayer we reaffirm that we accept G-d as our king, meaning that we submit to the grand plan for which the universe was created. These concepts are closer to a mind meditation than a declaration of actions we are prepared to take. Instead, we attempt to mentally prepare ourselves to achieve the purpose for which all humans were created. We will do this by resolving to live a life in the year to follow that allows us to develop our talents and we intend that this unfolding of inherent talents intersects with God's unknown purpose for creation. Rosh Hashana is the meditation part of the first rule of monotheism- one must trust in G-d and believe in positive outcomes.

While we pray for all of humankind we must include our people, our family and ourselves. We have a tradition that any prayer that does not include oneself and one's people is a prayer that is surely not heard. It was told to me that each person must meditate and prepare a list of inherent talents one hopes to unfold in the coming year. Simultaneously, one needs to prepare for an expectation of divine assistance in achieving this accomplishment. The most direct method of preparing for divine assistance is to enumerate how and where this help is needed i.e.. Good health, Divine inspiration, and guidance, precise measures that need to be taken, etc.

Yom Kippur

After Rosh Hashana the text lists the Yom Kippur Offering (*Numbers* 29:7(. In order to understand Yom Kippur we must continue the exercise where we compare Hagar to Abraham. Whereas Rosh Hashana focused on the first Monotheistic rule, Yom Kippur focuses on the second monotheistic rule- humankind is not impotent, we are empowered to act and create change even when the Rosh Hashana decree is not favorable.. Hagar did not believe that a human could take actions that are able to successfully intercede or affect the decree of the gods. Abraham, in contrast, was interested as an empowered individual to confront obstacles and resolve challenges to achieve his objective.

We, as humans, can effect a change in the heavenly plan. This is something that would have been unheard of to a pagan. Hagar saw the apparent decision of the gods as immutable without pagan spells and sorcery. Hagar intended to abandon Ishmael believing he must have failed to perform a ritual correctly which triggered the wrath of the gods. To her, the removal of both Ishmael and herself from Abraham's household, the sickness that now weakened Ishmael, and the lack of water were all the result of Ishmael's failure to properly serve and appease the gods. Even though she had received the blessing that her child would grow to become a great nation from the "god of seeing", she did not raise her voice to ask the god to somehow protect this blessed child. To Hagar's pagan mentality the promises where made by a mercurial god who was offended by Ishmael's actions. Ishmael's own actions doomed him regardless of all previous promises. The text shows us that she already lamented the death of her child although by just searching there was water still available to her. Her trauma and pagan beliefs prevented her from seeing the solution that she only had to lift her eyes to see.

If Yom Kippur was only about contrition and forgiveness, we would need to explain why any other day is not as good a day for contrition and forgiveness. Yom Kippur must have a special quality. Our sages have identified Yom Kippur as unique because it allows us to celebrate humankind as powerful beings who by their own exertion can change the fate that was determined on Rosh Hashana. "The annual decree is written on Rosh Hashana but sealed on Yom Kippur (*Nasanah Tokef* prayer)"

This stands in contrast to Hagar. In the Rosh Hashana Torah reading, as we already pointed out, she was unable on her own to see the solution in front of her. Due to her beliefs, she was impotent and refused to exert herself when facing a crisis levied by the gods. Thus, she needed the angel to open her eyes so she could see a solution that was clearly visible. Yom Kippur stands opposed to this pagan mentality. We declare that G-d has given mankind the power to effect a change and modify his fate. By an act of self-denial, on a single day, a person can modify G-d's Rosh Hashana decree. This empowers humankind to craft their personal lives to achieve the goals they are striving for. In polytheistic cultures humans are unable to effect change once decreed by the gods. They would doubt that the children of Abraham are given the power, via Yom Kippur, to effect G-d's decree and achieve "kapara", without any priestly intervention.

In conclusion, with the help of archeology, we understood how Hagar remained a pagan, although she continued living in the camp of Abraham. We identified the differences between Hagar's perception of the world and Abraham's. We then applied those differences to contrast between monotheism and polytheism. We focused on two examples that highlight this difference. The examples were derived from the Rosh Hashana scriptural reading. They became the key to unlocking the meaning of our observance of Rosh Hashana (a meditation on living an optimistic life) and Yom Kipur (an active dynamic experience that empowers humankind to effect change). Over the years the high holy days have been analyzed and much has been written in learned books and spoken from auspices pulpits. However, until we uncovered the true basics of its origin, we were forced to ascribe emotional meaning into what is the Bible's very powerful statement about monotheism.

Simply put, the High Holy Days are a declaration of monotheism and gives the Jews the opportunity to celebrate the core principles of monotheism. Judaism is based on the concept that the world was made for mankind to thrive. This first statement is made via a meditation (Rosh Hashana) and is couched in awesome praise to the the King of the Universe who is guiding humankind to a purpose. The second statement is made via an active tool (Yom Kippur) that demands humankind to rise, appreciate their inherent importance, and even alter the decree of G-d.

High Holy Days -Sukkoth

1. Why do we include Sukkoth in the midst of our New Years's celebration?

2. What are we to learn from the Torah referring to future generations as the reason why we are commanded to sit in the Sukkah? No other festival has their purpose being to inform future generations.

"In order that your [ensuing] generations should know that I had the children of Israel live in booths when I took them out of the land of Egypt. I am the Lord, your God." (*Leviticus* 23:43)

We are never told to do a directive i.e. Eating matza, observing Shabbat, so that future generations should be aware of a historical fact. What is the reason for this exceptional directive at Sukkoth?

3. It appears that we sit in a Sukkah as a commemoration of temporary housing. Surely there were other aspects of the *Exodus* that we can honor that better reflect the momentous act of taking out a nation from within a larger,

more powerful nation. Why does the Torah select the Sukkah experience?

Answer

As explained above, by contrasting the Sumerian culture to the Biblical creed we are made more aware of the Bible's intention to oppose the dehumanizing beliefs of polytheism. Whereas the Sumerian elites were telling the people that they were worthless, and their only purpose was to serve the gods the Bible was giving a positive message, uplifting humankind as the purpose of creation.

This Abrahamic belief in monotheism was manifested within the rituals of the High Holy Days. This celebration of mankind's unique relationship with G-d is continued by the Sukkoth observance. We are commanded to celebrate the generation of the *Exodus*, that lived in booths while on the journey to Canaan. The text tells future generations to point our focus away from all the ancient progenitors to another generation, that "greatest" generation that lived in the Sukkah on the way to Canaan. It is not the Sukkah itself that we are commemorating but the "greatest generation" that we are celebrating. This is indeed Judaism's "greatest generation." They were born in servitude, brought the first Pascal sacrifice, crossed the Reed sea, ate Manah, and completed the Brit Bain Habasorim (BBH). The Torah is asking every generation to honor that generation. We, as Jews, give homage to greatness by trying to emulate the greatness we are honoring. We cannot hope to recreate any of the grand accomplishments of Judaism's greatest generation. However, the Torah gives us a sliver of their lives that we can simulate and thereby honor the entirety of their amazing lives. The purpose of staying in the Sukah is not to focus on the living accommodations of the desert transit to Canaan, instead, we are meant to focus on the people who lived at the time of the *Exodus*, the Jewish people's greatest generation. This religious celebration commemorating human beings would have been blasphemy to the Sumerian pagans. To the pagan mind, only the gods can be celebrated, humans are not worthy of honor.

We can find some hints that we are commanded to emphasize the people of the exodus and not some spiritual connection to the Sukkah itself from the tradition of inviting the "Ushpizon" into the Sukkah. These are nightly guests that represent the greatest Jewish personalities i.e. Abraham, Isaak, Jacob, Moses, Aaron, and Joseph. We are gathering them into the Sukkah to honor great Biblical figures just like we gather in the Sukkah to honor the greatest generation.

In Sumerian culture, the experience of the common people was unimportant and would never have been glorified. Humans were tolerated but never loved by the gods. In contrast, The High Holy Days began with a proclamation of G-d's love for humankind and continues that theme in the weeks that follow by honoring a generation that became the Jewish people's greatest generation. The Bible once again stands diametrically opposed to the pagan diminution of humankind and the glorification of the Elites.

Shavuot

1. " And you shall remember that you were a slave in Egypt, and you shall keep and perform these statutes. (*Deuteronomy* 16:10)" The directive to observe Shavuot, commands us to remember that we were slaves in Egypt. We are not commanded to remember the miracles of the *Exodus* but instead, we are commanded to remember our enslavement. The Israelite enslavement in Egypt was unique. It was exceptional in that the servant-to-master relationship often results in the servant class being absorbed into the masters' culture, for example Egyptian society and Egyptian idolatry; This has occurred with countless other slaves and captives throughout human history. The Torah seems to want us to identify and celebrate the fact that the Israelites were able to stay separate and not be like so many other slaves who were drawn into their master's culture. So how does Shavuot, with its dearth of rituals, allow us to remember our enslavement in Egypt?

2. Why does Shavuot have this build-up of a seven-week counting commandment?

3. Why did the rabbis institute the reading of Megillat Ruth on Shavuot? It seems to be a story about the origins of King David. Could there be a hidden message?

Answer Upon reflection of the first question we understand that the Torah in *Deuteronomy* is asking us to remember the factors that allowed us to remain Israelites during our enslavement in Egypt. Some beliefs or behaviors prevented us from being absorbed into the most powerful and greatest culture of its day. When we start the search for the factors that kept us apart from Egyptian culture, we look at what hints the Bible reveals to us. It's a short list.

1. Firstly, the name Shavuot which simply means "weeks" tells us that this holiday is celebrating something to do with a unique time span. A week cannot be determined by the rotation of the earth that measures a day or the orbit of the moon dertermines the month. Weeks are a socially accepted mode of dividing up a month into sections. In ancient Sumer this was the purview of the temple priests. After Abraham, it was a continuous cycle of seven consecutive day groupings.

2. Then we have the counting of the Omer which leads up to the holiday. A cycle of seven weeks leads us almost like a bridal path to the holiday.

This seven-week cycle composed of seven-day weeks reminds us of the powerful tool Abraham gifted the world. In order to break the stranglehold that the pagan temples had on the masses, Abraham created the weekly cycle. When one week ends another week automatically begins. While this seems so normal to us today, we forget that there was a time when weeks did not automatically cycle one after the other. At a pre-Abrahamic time in Sumeria, it was the temple priests who divided up the months into four weeks. The Temple priests determined when the first day of the lunar month began. They viewed weeks as segments of their monthly announcements.

The priests told their believers that the seventh, fourteenth, nineteenth, twenty- first, and twenty- ninth day of every month was a cursed day and there were to be no celebrations or holidays on those days. With the innovation of the cyclical week, Abraham prevented the Temple priest from dictating when the week began (*The Genius of Abraham*, p. 70). People no longer needed the Temple to determine the new moon and then have a priest segment the new month into weeks. This process was now automatic and acted to break the control the Temple had on people's daily lives.

A calendar of continuous weeks was one of the tools to prevent assimilation that Abraham included in the toolbox of laws and ideas that he prepared when he was told at the Brit Bain Habasorim "... that your descendants will be foreigners in a land that is not theirs for four hundred years. They will be enslaved and oppressed"(*Genesis* 15:13). Ultimately. the gift of the cycle of weeks enabled us to remain apart from the Egyptian culture. While Egypt turned to its priestly class to determine the weeks of the month. The Israelites had a continuous cycle of weeks that repeated for eternity. It is this gift of Abraham that we celebrate on Shavuot. There were certainly many other tools in Abraham's survival toolbox, and they too would be celebrated on Shavuot.

For example, the law of "Do not cook meat in milk," that might have originally been another tool to show the barbarism of the Sumerian temples, is remembered by the inclusion of dairy meals on Shavuot.

By only selecting a single example of a much bigger picture is a method of honoring the bigger picture. Although we honor just the setting of the weekly cycle, we thereby honor the whole toolbox that kept Israel separate during their sojourn in Egypt.

We have now answered the first two questions and by continuing the same theme we can answer the third question. Now that we know that Shavuot is a tribute to Abraham's non-assimilation toolbox we can see the many parallels between Ruth and Abraham. In fact, the language Boaz (her future husband) uses to describe Ruth is almost identical to the Bible's language describing Abraham receiving the command to leave his father's home, the land of his birth, to go to Canaan. Clearly reading the story of Ruth on Shavuot is a tribute to both Abraham and Ruth. Both followed their destinies to the land of Canaan, where the Jewish people stand as a light unto the nations. May those who commemorate the efforts of our father Abraham, to ensure that the Israelites endured their captivity in Egypt be rewarded with the many blessings that Abraham received for trusting in G-d.

I feel a need to end this second book by addressing those of us who are fortunate to have the faith that our lives are being led to an existential objective. Although we can't yet sing the song or perform the dance. In these precarious times, the faithful should be confident that the stage is nearly set. On that note I present the following essay.

Essay: Ninth of Av (the gift of hope)

On the 9th of Av, the Jews commemorate the destruction of the temple nearly 2000 years ago. Since that time, we have suffered the horrors of the Nazi Holocaust. It is important to point out the differences between these two events. The destruction of the temple occurred during the Roman conquest of the state of Judah. Prior to that destruction, on the same calendar day 656 years earlier, the first Temple was destroyed by the armies of Babylon. In both cases, there was a normal process of one empire subjugating a smaller country and taking over its cities and holy places. This willful destruction was done methodically and repeatedly in many other countries that were conquered by these Empires. However, the Holocaust had a different component. It wasn't a case where one country was conquering another country and killing off its population. Instead, it was selecting the Jewish residents of the invaded country to intentionally humiliate, dehumanize, and murder the Jewish people who were living in the borders of the conquered state. These Jews were often citizens of the countries they were residing in. They even fought in wars to defend and protect the governments of these countries. Dehumanizing the Jews was an important component of the Nazi program. What is so ironic about the dehumanization of the Jewish people, is that our father, Abraham, is revered for bringing monotheism to the world. Monotheism views each human being as being made in the image of G-d and possessing innate dignity to pray directly to G-d and is expected to view life as an opportunity to grow and to reach his or her potential. Hitler sought to dehumanize the Jews, and Abraham tried to elevate all of humanity. We can easily state that Abraham stood for dignity and good while Hitler was the antithesis of Abraham. The Nazi was precisely the evil opposite of the good that Abraham stood for, the elevation of people. This contrast is important to stress since it creates a category of extreme behavior that will allow us to grasp the meaning of Biblical verses that have puzzled scholars for generations.

We have a timeline with the Bris Bain Habasorim as a monument to G-d's love for Abraham followed by a fourteen-years span until the Brit Milah. Sadly, we have an example of the polar opposite of Abraham, Hitler becoming the fuhrer of Germany, followed by a fourteen-year span until the establishment of the State of Israel.

We emphasize that there were 14 years between the Bris bane Habasorim and the Brit Mila in comparison to the 14 years between 1934 when Hitler was declared the fuhrer of Germany and 1948 when the state of Israel was established.

For centuries scholars have pondered the enigmatic meaning of two verses in the Bible.

We can now turn to these incredible verses in *Genesis* 17. We read in verse # 7 :

וַהֲקִמֹתִי אֶת־בְּרִיתִי בֵּינִי וּבֵינֶךָ וּבֵין זַרְעֲךָ אַחֲרֶיךָ לְדֹרֹתָם לִבְרִית עוֹלָם לִהְיוֹת לְךָ לֵהִי וּלְזַרְעֲךָ אַחֲרֶיךָ:

"I will sustain my covenant between me and between you and your descendants after you throughout their generations an eternal covenant: I will be a G-d to you and to your offspring after you, and the next verse *Genesis* 17:8 says "to you and your offspring I will give the land where you are now living, as a foreigner; The whole land of Canaan shall be your eternal heritage and I will be a G-d to your descendants"

ונתתי לך ולזרעך אחריך את ארץ מגריך את כל ארץ כנען לאחזת עולם וְהָיִיתִי לָהֶם לֵהִי

The question is why it is necessary to repeat again, "I will be a G-d to your descendants." Both in verse number 7 and then again in verse number 8, G-d states" I will be a god to your descendants' and Rashi seeks to understand the purpose of the repetition. He creates a dichotomy between the event of the BBH and an event that will happen in the future. Both are promised "I will be a G-d to you and your offspring after you."

Living in modern times and referring to our timeline above we can answer this age-old question. As stated above, When we pin moments in Jewish history that consist of extreme good and extreme evil i.e. The good is Abraham, experiencing the Bris Bain Habasorim and the evil is the antithesis of Abraham, Hitler, becoming fuhrer in 1934. Both are followed by a fourteen-year gap that leads to a monumental moment for the Jewish people. We are creating this parallel between Abraham's 14-year gap which was then followed by the Brit Milah and the bond of "I will be a G-d to you and to your offspring after you."

The repetition in the next verse, according to Rash, refers to a time, when the Jewish nation will again reside in Canaan when that exact timeline is repeated i.e. an Abrahamic event (or has unfortunately happened the anti-Abrahamic event, the Holocaust), followed by 14-year hiatus to the next great Jewish moment, the establishment of the state of Israel. G-d promises **"I will be a G-d to your descendants."** Rashi explains that the Torah is emphasizing, at that time in history when the Jewish people have returned to the land, then I will reveal my closeness to you. The children of Abraham had not been forgotten, we were never forgotten, even on the cattle cars to Treblinka and Auschwitz. The horrors of the Nazis concluded centuries of degradation of the Jewish people. During those dark times, G-d was allowing history to play out while He was waiting for His people to return to Zion. The prophecy that was given at Sinai is being witnessed only in modern times. Now, we are here in Zion, fear not, you are under His care and protection as we read in Scripture,

"The whole land of Canaan shall be your eternal heritage and I will be a G-d to your descendants."

The stage is nearly set. The Jewish nation has returned to its eternal heritage. We must not fear the serious threats that constantly arise to harm the survival of the state of Israel. Since we trust that as verse 8 states, "I will be a G-d to your descendants." We live our lives in Israel with joy and gladness, knowing we are protected.

It may at first seem strange to end this book with an analysis of the fast day called the Ninth of Av. However, since it includes the prophecy found in *Genesis* 17:8, a powerful prophecy that applies to our times. G-d's promise of "when they return to Canaan, I will be a G-d to your descendants" This promise gives us a positive message of hope and safety. Maybe it will encourage those who can, to consider moving to Israel.

Endnotes

1   We can trace Abraham's distaste for monarchy as reflected in his concern when Sarah is twice taken by monarchs for their harems. He distrusts Monarchs. He feels that their sense of entitlement would permit them to kill him if it meant they could keep Sarah.

We can also find limits to the Monarchy's power in the Torah's laws. Unlike Sumerian tradition, Torah laws do not require a king in order for the prayers of the people to be heard. Of course, in the Biblical tradition, dead kings are never deified as was the custom in Mesopotamia. The Torah put restrictions on Jewish kings to force them to focus on national defense and prevent them from waging wars for glorious conquests, which was the fashion of the time. Abraham not trusting monarchy doesn't mean he is unwilling to engage with them if it helps bring people to monotheism.

2   Interestingly, just like the Sodomites, the Israelites would experience the exact same circumstances prior to Sinai. Specifically, the Israelites were recently freed from bondage and also had no king. Even Moses, who was a prophet and a leader was not a king. A king would have the rules of heredity that assured the kingship of his progeny. Moses was unable to transfer his position to his children. Yet Israelites went on to accept Judaism and the Sodomites reverted to paganism.

Abraham will eventually learn that the Sodomites never followed the path of "doing tzedakah" and justice and consequently they descended into depravity. However, Abraham's descendants have an alternate ending. The Bible tells us "I have given him special attention so that he will command his children and his household after him, and they will keep G-d's way, "doing tzedakah and justice."(*Genesis* 1:17) Although Abraham's efforts with Sodom proved useless, he will try again to influence the residents of Canaan with a "well" Strategy (see chapter 9).

3   It is possible the tradition for the bride and groom to drink from the same glass under the marriage canopy stands as a reminder of our Sumerian roots. It was expected, that at the cere-

monial dinner, the Suzerain and Vassal would drink from the same cup (F. Joannes, Marchands, Diplomates et Empereurs (Paris, Editions Recherches sur les Civilisations, A.D.P.F.,1991, n.27).

4   A common issue that is often raised is why Abraham never raises a complaint to G-d that his children should be spared slavery. To possibly understand his behaviour, I would like to suggest the following. Archeology has uncovered that when Abraham was in Ur, the city was recently freed from Akkadian hegemony which ruled over Ur for approximately two hundred and fifty years. The freedom of Ur resulted in the flowering of Sumerian creativity and innovation during what archeologists refer to as the Third Dynasty of Ur. Is it possible that Abraham learned that the human mind achieves maximum creativity when de-stressed from hegemony, slavery, or any other form of mental suppression? We can actually find examples of this in recent history. The highly creative Jews who founded Hollywood and its many studios were often escapees of Russian Tzarist oppression. Another example is the amazing, highly creative minds of the Russian immigrants who came to Israel and enabled Israel to become a start-up nation. Could Abraham understand from observing his own city that his children would need to endure slavery in order to achieve maximum creativity? They would need this creativity to sustain their belief as a nation of monotheists in a pagan world.

Although technically Abraham did not complete the Suzerain-Vassal Treaty by walking down the aisle made by the cut animals of the BBH, God declares "By myself, I have sworn (*Genesis* 21:16). Thus, the agreement moves forward even without Abraham's direct participation in the completion of the Suzerain-Vassal Treaty.

5   The most obvious difference between the Britot is the move from Abraham having a universal calling to influence and convert the entire world. This original mission is changed to a more personal relationship with G-d, at the Brit Milah. This new mission centers on Abraham and his progeny, we can see this change when the Lord uses the intimate term Baynei Ubane'cha (between me and you). At the Bris Milah, Abraham is redirected to focus on influencing his "Zerah". This can be seen in the promises

made at the Brit Milah. The text says "I will be to them (Abraham's Zerah) for a G-d" (*Genesis* 17:8) This intimate promise was not previously mentioned and is happening now because the mission has changed from the universal to the personal. This special relationship will require the observance of Torah laws.

This stipulation of observing Torah laws is not mentioned at Brit Milah and only becomes apparent later on when Isaak receives inducements to stay in Canaan and not journey to Egypt. After Abraham's death, and due to a famine in Canaan, Isaak is considering visiting Egypt. G-d appears to him and offers inducements for him to stay in Canaan. Suddenly we read that G-d had not only modified the scope of the mission at the Brit Milah but had also altered the obligation on the children of Abraham to be worthy of the promise of "I will be a G-d to you and your offspring after you"(*Genesis* 17:7). The fulfillment of the promise and the blessings are dependent on observing commandments, statutes, and laws.

Until now the only requirement for getting the land of Canaan promised at the Brit Milah was circumcision, now for the first time we are told that in order to obtain the fulfillment of the blessings it also requires the observance, by the children of Abraham, of an entire collection of laws.

Does the text tell us that G-d is only willing to continue the previously made covenants if the Torah laws are observed? Adding on additional and previously unmentioned conditions after Abraham's circumcision would be an illegal breach of the covenant. Once a covenant is enacted additional conditions can no longer be added.

This legal hurdle is not an issue for the following reason. There was a representation at the time of the Brit Milah that Abraham was a "Tamim." G-d is telling Isaak that He seeks that those who continue the covenant must also continue to act as a "Tamim." The sudden mention of the laws is not an additional stipulation to the treaty. The laws are a psychological method to mold a person into having an intimate relationship with G-d and thereby becoming a "Tamim." This is necessary since the land of Canaan was given to a Tamim. The "Tamim" quality must continue onto future generations in order for the treaty to remain intact. Only by trusting that

G-d directs the life of each person to achieve positive predetermined outcomes, can a person become a "Tamim." We know this from the lesson Abraham receives when he is told to look at the stars and then told that although he can see some stars, he can't see the whole universe. This is where Abraham learns that there is a universal divine plan and as a monotheist, he must trust that the Creator is leading humankind to a predetermined outcome.

Where to now? How do we achieve this elusive goal? Can one observe all the laws of the Torah and still not trust in positive predetermined outcomes?

Maybe the question is the answer. The Bible does not give us the definitive recipe for becoming a Tamim because for each person the equation is different. Becoming a Tamim is a goal. Which road we choose to take is up to each individual.

Having a bond with the Lord is a criterion for a belief in positive outcomes. The mindset of "a belief in positive outcomes", was the very nature of Abraham himself. When the children of Abraham achieve this mindset, they too are in the covenant. The observance of Torah laws, doing "tzadakah" and justice, is done for the purpose of creating a bond with G-d. That bond sets a framework for a person to become a Tamim and consequently part of the covenant.

Living in the twenty-first century gives us a unique opportunity to witness what happens when sincere good-hearted people try to do tzadakah and justice but fail to use it to bond with G-d. Instead, they use their efforts to bond with socialism, humanism, and globalism. In the end, their efforts will bring unimaginable fear and misery to themselves and the people they were trying to help. People of faith understand that we strive to be like Abraham with the goal of adopting his trust in positive outcomes.

From God's perspective, once Abraham brought a belief in positive outcomes to the negotiating table it became part of the Brit. Requiring the continuance of that mindset is not a new stipulation It is just a clarification of what is required for the fulfillment of the blessings based on the fact it was present from the very first Bris Bain Habasorim

6   Now we must ask ourselves - How did Abraham perceive the request to offer up his son as a sacrifice?

At this point in his life, Abraham is dealing with three depressing factors hitting at the same time. They are as follows:

The text separated the Brit Bain Habasorim from the Brit Milah with the story of Hagar and the birth of Ishmael. Previously, in Chapter 5, we showed how we concluded, based on her interaction with the "seeing" angel, that she was still a polytheist. Hagar and Ishmael remain pagans even when living in Abraham's house. We concluded that the reason for the Bible to include the Hagar story between the two Brits was to elucidate the cause for the change in Abraham's outlook from one Brit to the next. We determined the story of Hagar was pointing to the cause for Abraham's mood swing to a broken heart. There seemed to be a temporary move to optimism when G-d continued the Suzerain-Vassal Treaty by changing his and Sari's name.

We read about his mood improvement when he was willing to include Ishmael in the Brit Milah covenant. The Torah makes special mention of Ishmael's Brit. This separate sentence is significant since Abraham was already commanded to circumcise all the members of his household which should have included Ishmael. It may be teaching us that considering Ishmael's behavior, Abraham could have intentionally excluded Ishmael from the Brit. The text tells us that by including Ishmael, Abraham expected all his children would be monotheists. However, it is years later, and Sarah has caught Ishmael continuing to practice idolatry and insists Abraham evict both mother and child. Only reluctantly does Abraham agree.

Now we will look into Scripture to find additional factors Abraham was contending with. Alongside, the eviction of Hagar and Ishmael, the Bible relates a story of Abimelech and Pichol (*Genesis* 21:22) coming to make a treaty with Abraham (see chapter 3). In addition to a payment for a disputed well, a multi-generational peace treaty was organized. The text doesn't state that the treaty fails to be completed when Abimelech leaves prior to the required joint meal, which nullifies the treaty (*Genesis* 21:32). We only know the treaty failed because Isaak needs to recut the treaty after his father passes away (*Genesis* 26:30). This time the treaty is finally enacted when Abimelech and Pichol stay for the meal. The inability to complete a common treaty probably added to Abraham's sense of sadness.

Finally, Scripture gives us a third factor weighing on Abraham at this time. Although he negotiates for Sodom, he is unable to save them from their fate.

This is truly his darkest hour. Abraham was unable to convert the pagans of Canaan, Ishmael, and Hagar were evicted from his home, his efforts to save Sodom were ineffective and he was even unable to make a political treaty with Abimelech (king of Gerar). Amid all this sadness he is determined to complete the Binding of Isaak. At every stage of the journey to Moriah, we are reminded of Abraham's sincerity and obedience. He gets up early to fulfill his tasks, he doesn't question G-d's request, and he travels for several days to reach his destination without turning back. Abraham doesn't tell Isaak of the plan until they arrive at MT. Moriah. Once there, he projects onto Isaak, a trust in G-d that he is confident Isaak, like himself, has. Isaak does agree. This cooperative/ supportive behavior by Isaak is therapeutic to Abraham's depressed mind. Abraham has an ally! This is another step in his recovery.

The character of an individual is revealed when we see how they act under severe pressure. Although under extreme stress, Abraham still has the internal strength to see the world outside of himself and does an act of kindness. He does this by protecting the attendants, who accompanied him and Isaak, from possible harm. He asks them to stay behind, away from the sacrificial altar, he will construct on Mount Moriah. He is concerned for their safety, while he is sure Isaak will be spared because of the promises made by G-d he does not yet know how Isaak will be saved; he is asking them to stay a day's journey behind so that none of the attendants can be substituted for Isaak.

In further recognition of Abraham's "trust", when Abraham is asked to kill Isaak, the child whom G-d had promised would be the one to fulfill the many promises of "seed" and "land"(*Genesis* 15:4), he is surely despondent, yet he stays silent. Clearly, it is the confidence that Isaak will not be sacrificed that keeps him silent.

7   The concept of Hineni (I am here) is often discussed as Abraham showing complete obedience but given our understand-

ing of Abraham's state of mind, we need to reassess the Hineni term as used by Abraham when responding to the Lord's call at the Binding of Isaak.

We are in an endless search to better understand Abraham's motivations. Since Hineni was part of the Binding of Isaak can we look to extract some insight as to why we hear Hineni for the first time at the this second Lech Lacha?

We will first try contrasting the two Lech Lacha's that G-d directed to Abraham.There are direct comparisons between Lech Lacha at the instruction for Abraham to leave Haran and Lech Lacha at the binding of Isaak. Both are instances of Abraham having unquestioned faith in G-d. In both cases, Abraham goes to a non-defined place because he obeys the "go" command without knowing where his "going" is leading. At Haran and at the binding of Isaak in Canaan, Abraham is willing to "go" without being told were. Abraham is willing to take on whatever challenge lies ahead. Is this, boundless faith, represented by Hineni?

Maybe the motivation for Abraham saying Hineni when he is called by G-d after the Brit Milah is not the same response as the optimistic Abraham of the BBH. He might actually be saying-" I have done all I can do on my own. Now I turn to you, my Lord, to lead me back to health." For Abraham, it is a term of resignation of the self and the acceptance that only through divine providence will there be a solution. "Hineni" is therefore not necessarily the ideal example of boundless faith by a person who seeks to bind himself to a belief in positive outcomes. It might be the voice of the desperate seeking relief. We also find that Esau (*Genesis* 27:1) uses the Hineni term when speaking to his father.

In conclusion, Abraham's following the Lech Lacha command at the Binding of Isaak was seemingly an example of boundless faith. However, based on the above analysis, we cannot prove Abraham's boundless faith by his use of the term "Hineni." Furthermore, even though the term Hineni does not help us understand Abraham's boundless faith we know from *Genesis* (26:5) that the mitzvot are meant to lead us into a relationship with G-d and thereby achieve this elusive objective.

8   An important life lesson we can glean from Abraham and Sarah's failed efforts is that although Abraham and Sarah had concocted a plan to convert the Elites of Canaan and Egypt, they were sabotaged, not by folly but by the Lord's plague. Before they could implement their plan, a plague was brought upon both Pharaoh and Abimelech. Abraham and Sarah had planned to fulfill G-d's command to leave Haran and proselytize in Canaan, why would G-d sabotage this effort?

We can learn from this that even attempting with the sincerest efforts to do truth and justice does not guarantee success. The "grand" plan is hidden from all, even Abraham and Sarah. It was explained to me that we are all on personal journeys, and so are countries and nations. Since Abraham's plan extended to affect a nation via its royal household. The result could have been the establishment of a state religion. This may have exceeded Abraham's mission to convert individuals to monotheism. There may be a Biblical preference to have a definite separation of state religion from personal worship. Only Israel as the bastion of monotheism has its state religion and spiritual individuals on the same track. May it be blessed.

9   Let's review the verses that are recorded when the angels sit down with Abraham:

They asked him, "Where is your wife, Sarah?" (*Genesis* 18:9) They are really asking, "Where is the bread she was asked to prepare?" The angels are confirming that Sarah's strategy could indeed sabotage the Brit Milah, without the bread this meal will not conclude the Brit Milah. Abraham responds, "Here in the tent" (ibid.18:9). In other words, she has no intention of baking the required bread, baking was done outside in kilns not inside the tents. Regardless of her behavior, the angel promises Abraham, "I will return to you this time next year and your wife, Sarah, will have a son."(*Genesis* 18:10). The angel stays focused on Sarah and the next words the angel speaks is also about Sarah, "Why did Sarah laugh<tzahakah> and say, 'Can I really have a child when I am so old' Is anything too difficult for G-d? At the designated time, I will return, and Sarah will have a son." (ibid.1:13,14) We translate the "tzahok" as laugh. However, that was clearly not what Sarah actually did. According to the text, she only repeated the same amazement that Abraham expressed when he was told during the Brit Milah the same information. "She laughed<Va titzhak> to herself, saying 'Now that I am worn out, shall I have my heart's desire? My husband is old'"(ibid.18:12)

We find the same word Vayitzhok was used to describe Abraham's response, "Abraham fell on his face, and he laughed<Va'yitzhok>. He said to himself, 'Can a hundred-year-old man have children? Can Sarah, who is ninety, give birth'?"(*Genesis* 17:17). Rabbinic sources go even further to emphasize that Sarah was not doubting G-d's abilities, Rashi writes that Sarah was actually entertaining the idea of having a pregnant woman's smooth skin. The simple reading of the text is problematic. What exactly were the angels' charges against her? They falsely claimed she said things she didn't say, then they belittled her for saying words that she never implied. What is going on here?

To begin to unravel this we will first need to define the term "tzachok" Previously we showed how all the stories from the BBH through the Binding of Isaac, which includes this story, are part of a legal contract giving the children of Abraham and Isaak the land of Canaan. This insight comes to us from archeology that revealed the many steps of the Suzerain-Vassal Treaty.

We can now explain that when the word "tzahok" is being used by the angel, it is legal terminology comparable to the legal term, "material breach." A "material breach", which in American jurisprudence refers to some deficiency that prevents a legal procedure from progressing directly due to a legal condition not being fulfilled. Having different meanings for the word "Tzahok" is not radical. We find the word "Tzahok" sprinkled throughout this section of the Bible.

When Ishmael is caught worshiping idols.(*Genesis* (21:9)
When Abraham is told he will have a son (ibid.17:17)
When Sarah overhears that she will give birth (ibid.18:12)
When Sarah names Isaak (ibid.21:6)

At each mention the word has a different meaning. Therefore, to suggest the word has a legal meaning when Sarah is accused of "tzachok" is not radical.

"Is anything too difficult for G-d?" (ibid.18:14). The angel is rhetorically asking Abraham why has Sarah sabotaged the Brit Milah by not baking the bread? She is wrong to think G-d is subject to earthly conventions, specifically the technicalities of Sumerian covenants. "At the designated time, I will return, and Sarah will have a son" (ibid.18:13).

The angel then repeats, for emphasis, after already stating it just three verses earlier that there will be a son born to Sarah. The angel is assuring Abraham that the covenant moves forward regardless of Sarah's reluctance to bake the bread. Her behavior does not terminate the treaty of Milah. The birth of Isaak verifies the covenant of Milah, even without a concluding meal.

"Sarah was afraid, and she denied it. 'I did not laugh,' she said" (ibid.18:15) When questioned, as to why she sabotaged the Brit; she was afraid that Ishmael might grow violent knowing that Sarah blocked his blessings that was included in the Brit Milah. So afraid of explaining her behavior she disingenuously answers that I did not intentionally sabotage the Brit Milah. "And he said 'You did laugh'" (ibid.18:15). She is then told the attempt to sabotage the covenant of the Milah, has been attributed to her. This should be understood as another complement to her commitment to monotheism.

When the angel asks Abraham why Sarah is (tzachok) they are not implying that Sarah was mocking G-d's ability to grant her a child. The angel is referring to the portion of the Brit Milah that relates directly to Sarah, the promise of her having a child, and asking about her actions to sabotage the Brit (by not baking the bread). Thus, she is not being questioned about her thoughts but about her not baking the bread. This resolves the contradiction between what she thought and what she was being accused of.

Rashi's explanation of the next sentence "Is anything hidden from Hashem" confirms our analysis. The Torah uses the term "Hayipoleh" which usually means amazement, which would have been an appropriate word to be used to describe the pregnancy of a ninety-year-old woman. However, Rashi, in the Rabbinic tradition defines the word as hidden.

This supports our contention that Sarah is doing something that she thinks is hidden from G-d and she can stay in her tent to keep the matter hidden. Namely, her actions are working to surreptitiously void the Brit Milah treaty. The angel is telling her that one cannot hide from the Lord. She responds to the accusation by saying I did not "tzachok" and the angel responds you did" tzachok", meaning you did try to stop the covenant.

10 The hidden second story being unfolded in this chapter, is revealed to the modern reader because we now know from Sumerian archeology that there needed to be bread for the concluding meal that Sarah was told to prepare.

Although we explained the verses used by the angels, we now need to understand the cryptic verses stated by Sarah.

When the angels at Mamre repeat the promise made at the Brit Milah regarding the birth of Isaak, our ancient interpreters have expounded the following passage.

"Sarah was listening behind the entrance of the tent……. She laughed to herself saying 'Now that I am worn out, shall I have my heart's desire?(ibid.18:12)

While the Septuagint translation defines the word "ednah" as the heart's desire. The Rabbinic definition of "ednah" is skin smoothness (Rashi). The Rabbinic commentators are saying that upon rehearing about her upcoming pregnancy, Sarah is triggered to think about her skin regaining youthful smoothness. This seems strange that a ninety-year-old woman who has yearned for children her whole life when miraculously given the chance to have a child, would react by having concern about her skin tone. Also, when the angel accused Sarah of doubting G-d's power to have her birth a child, the reader knows, according to the Rabbinic tradition, that the angel got it completely wrong. There seems to be a disconnect between the stated thoughts that the Bible recorded and the angel's accusation.

We can now answer this disconnect. Based on the fact that she already knew from the Brit Milah, that she was going to have a child it is clear that her "private thoughts" had nothing to do with doubting G-d's power, as the angel accused. The only alternative is that Sarah fully accepts that she will have a child and is assessing the ramifications of her pregnancy. We know Sarah, the ultimate monotheist despises Hagar, the idolatress, who has become her archenemy. We discussed this intense disgust above. We should be able to point to Hagar as the object of Sarah's "mocking."

According to Sumerian law the primary wife, Sarah is entitled to rule over Hager even though Hagar has become Abraham's baby-making concubine. Furthermore, Isaak as the child of the primary wife will oust Ishmael as the inheritor of Abraham's estate and blessings. The Brit Milah confirms that only Isaak will inherit Abraham and this accords with Sumerian law as stated above - the child of the primary wife takes dominance over children born to concubines, even when the concubines' children are older. Sarah is rational to worry about Hagar and Ishmael.

Sarah has complained to Abraham that Hagar, has compared Sarah's appearance to that of an old woman (Aco-wild goat)

"When she<Hagar> realized that she was pregnant, she looked at her mistress with contempt" (*Genesis* 16:4). The term used for contempt is "Akal" which can also mean goat instead of the common term for contempt, m'va'ze.

So, when Sarah is contemplating the repercussions of the angel's prophesy, Sarah considers two results of the pregnancy and birth. First, she thinks about her expected improvement in appearance (I will be smooth again). Which will directly contradict Hagar's nasty comments. Sarah is committed to monotheism and fighting polytheism. Anytime she can prove an idolater wrong is a good day for Sarah.

 Sarah's second insight is regarding her relationship with Abraham. When Sarah thinks that her husband is old, Sarah, also an older person, is indicating she will rely on Abraham to assist in the job of raising Isaak. In addition to their proselytizing, they will do this job united as a team. The birth of Isaak will be a continuation of their joint efforts to bring monotheism to the world. Sarah's thought is not that she doubts that G-d will grant her a child at ninety. The angel knows this, and yet he continues to needle her because he has an agenda to complete the Brit Milah and is hoping to coerce Sarah into baking the bread. Sarah holds firm to her intention to block the covenant and doesn't bake the bread.

11   The Bible states that only because of fear did Sarah respond, "I did not tzachok." Let us unpack this response. We have

shown Sarah is fearful of a vengeful Hagar and Ishmael, who might try to prevent Ishmael from being excluded from any blessings. We arrived at this insight because Sarah when listening behind the tent wall hears about the prediction that she will have a child at ninety. The ancient interpreters explain that Sarah is thinking about her skin getting rejuvenated (Rashi on *Genesis* 18:12), Surprisingly, Sarah seems focused on her skin instead of the miracle of having a child at ninety. Obviously, we must conclude Sarah is actually focused on Hagar, who had previously commented on her goat-like skin (ibid.16:4).

Sarah has complained to Abraham that Hagar, has compared Sarah's appearance to that of an old woman (Aco-wild goat)

She relishes that Hagar, the idol worshipper, will be proven wrong. Sarah completely believes that indeed she will have a child, but as the mother of monotheism, her first response is that this pregnancy will mock the idol worshiping, Hagar. Being pregnant will result in her once again having the glow of smooth skin, which she sees as a refutation of Hagar's words. Sarah must have seen Hagar and her pagan son as her archenemies. When Sarah is accused of consciously voiding the Brit Milah, she responds out of fear. We are not told what she feared. Aware of this second background story we can confirm that Sarah is afraid of these pagans, as the Bible clearly states, she lies.

12   We can discover a possible reason for Sarah's sabotaging the Brit Milah. Sarah was challenging The Brit Milah because it did something the Bris Bain Habasorim did not do. It gave very specific blessings to Ishmael. "I have also heard you with regard to Ishmael. I will bless him and make him fruitful, increasing his numbers greatly. He will father twelve princes, and I will make him into a great nation." (*Genesis* 20). This triggers Sarah to react.

Prior to Ishmael's birth, Sarah has been arguing with Abraham about whether Hagar, the perennial pagan, should be allowed to stay under Abraham's tent. Sarah disagrees with Abraham's patience for idolaters and wants Hagar ousted from Abraham's tent. This might be the actual reason she says that G-d should judge between her and Abraham when she starts to react to Hagar's insolence (*Genesis* 16:5). Sarah wants G-d to advise them on whose approach is correct. Abraham's patient approach or Sarah's intolerant approach. When Ishmael is found idol worshiping after his circumcision, Abraham finally asks G-d and is told "Whatever Sarah tells you, in this case, hearken to her voice (ibid.21:12) . Sarah's intolerance regarding Hagar and Ishmael, pagans, who would not convert to monotheism although they were living in Abraham's house, must be evicted.

Sarah's reason for sabotaging the Brit Milah is a continuation of this theme. Sarah does not want the pagan, Ishmael, to inherit any of Abraham's possessions. This includes the blessings that began as inducements promised to Abram for leaving Haran. Sarah's conviction is resolute, pagans who have been exposed to monotheism and yet remain idolaters are not welcomed into Abraham's tent. She feels this way even though Isaak receives the bulk of the blessings and the entire land of Canaan. "Drive away this slave together with her son, The son of this slave will not share the inheritance with my son Issak." (ibid.21:10)

13   We can now understand why the Scripture is keen to explain that Sarah's denial of mocking the Bris Milah is because she is afraid. She is trying not to inflame Hagar & Ishmael by admitting to intentionally undermining the Brit Milah she says "I did not mock" meaning I did not intentionally undermine the Brit Milah. She is being told that she did try to block the Bris Milah from concluding. "You did block" the Brit and it is not yet completed. We have two hints that Sarah was convinced that she was able to permanently block the Bris Milah.

Instead of naming her child "Isaak" because Hashem promised her a child at the Bris Milah when Abraham was told to name the child Isaak; Sarah thinks his name is joyous because she had a child in her old age. "G-d has given me laughter. All who hear about it will laugh for me." (ibid.21:6) This strange disconnect is understandable if Sarah thought the Bris Milah was blocked and not in effect. It would also explain why Scripture uses the term to describe Isaac's Milah as a commandment instead of the fulfillment of a covenant. To Sarah, Milah is a commandment and not a sign of a covenant."When his son Isaak was eight days old, Abraham circumcised him, as G-d had commanded" (ibid.21:4)

14   In order for us to better understand Abraham's entering into a treaty that demands he upholds a belief in positive outcomes, we first need to understand the core beliefs of monotheism:
First core belief of monotheism:

Humankind is expected to "trust" that G-d is leading humankind to a world where humans can achieve the flowering of their innate and potential goodness. We can see this theme when Adam and Eve are originally placed in the Garden of Eden. They reside in a Garden where they do not need to work for their daily bread, nor are they challenged by disease, old age, or even the pangs of childbirth. Their sole purpose is to exist in harmony with nature, to respond to G-d's expectations of them, and to spend their days representing themselves as the pinnacle of earth's creation.

Adam is warned not to eat from the tree of knowledge. This is a very specific kind of knowledge. It is knowledge of good and evil. Practically speaking when there is evil in the world, humankind should be knowledgeable of this possible peril, so they can be careful to avoid the evil. When mankind was proscribed from the Tree of Knowledge and therefore avoided eating its fruit, humankind's survival must have relied on their Creator to keep them safe from evil. Since Adam and Eve did not have knowledge about evil, humankind had to trust in the Lord, that they were protected from any and all harm that could occur throughout their existence on the earth. The" fall of Adam" was not only the sin of transgressing G-d's command. It was also the arrogance of Adam refusing to trust that G-d would protect him from evil.

We find this theme, that mankind has an existential purpose to trust in the Lord, in another instance. At the start of the many exploits that the Bible recorded of Abraham's life in Canaan; Abraham is assured that he will father many children. He is told, as an analogy, to look up to the sky and count the stars. He is commanded to do something he humanly cannot do. Just standing in an open area and looking up does not make it possible to count the innumerable galaxies of stars. The very next words in the Bible confirm that the task is unachievable "See if you can count them <as the task is not able to be done>(*Genesis* 15:5). Abraham was instructed to accomplish a task that was beyond his capabilities and yet the next sentence begins "He trusted in the Lord" (ibid.15:6).

This is where we are told straight out that a monotheist is required to trust in the Lord especially when his human abilities are limited.

A second example, given at the very start of mankind will be given below. These examples reaffirm the contention that trusting in the Lord's plan for humankind is an integral part of the monotheistic experience.

Why would a creature be prevented from knowing the evil that could harm him? Isn't it wise to be aware of any peril before it happens? The real fall of Adam was that by seeking the knowledge of the evils that can befall mankind he was breaking the bond that G-d was prepared to guard him from all evil. It was a statement of rebellion. Adam was claiming that with knowledge of the evil in the world, he could face it himself and did not need to rely on G-d to protect him. Adam was exhibiting arrogance, but the Bible does not label it as such, instead, the Bible gives us an example of Adam's arrogance derived from his newly acquired knowledge. Adam assessed that being the pinnacle of creation he should be clothed in resplendent attire. Although he already clothed his nakedness, he still claims to be naked. Adam associates being under-dressed for his station as equivalent to being naked. Now we can better understand his punishment for eating from the tree of knowledge. His arrogance led him to eat from the tree of knowledge which then led to his being humbled. Adam's premise is that he is entitled to live a carefree existence in a garden that was designed to both nourish and delight him. G-d quickly erases any such notion by exiling him from Eden and requiring him to work for his daily bread. Eve's punishment of suffering the pangs of childbirth also reflects the humbling of her former arrogance that she can manipulate Adam without consequences. She too is humbled. However, as a loving parent, G-d first makes sure Adam and Eve are properly dressed in leather outfits that is practical for both work and warmth. Adam is told that whereas originally, he was to have a life of ease and comfort, he will now have a life of work and challenge.

We find further confirmation of the importance of trust in monotheism as the sentence continues "and it <trusting in the Lord> was credited to Abraham as fulfilling the "mitzvah of Tzadakah." By itself the segment of the sentence is enigmatic. However, when the reader proceeds to chapter 18:9 that "the path of the Lord is to do the Mitvah of Tzadakah and justice" it suddenly becomes clear. Abraham did the "Mitvah of Tzadakah" when he trusted in the Lord; something humans must adopt in order for the monotheist's future to unfold.

Second core belief of monotheism:

Monotheism demands that humanity is viewed as the pinnacle of creation. This understanding of humanity can lead to greater respect for all stages of human life. For some individuals, it empowers them to rise up and challenge any authority that tries to demean humanity, as did Abraham, when he challenged the elites of Sumer. This power to challenge can even be directed toward G-d. Abraham himself argues with G-d when told of the destruction of Sodom and Moses also argues with G-d when he is told that the Israelites will be destroyed in an instant (*Numbers* 17:9).

The ideal world is achieved when there is a universal understanding that G-d has given humankind the gift of life and each individual has the innate power of finding meaning in this world that was created for the specific purpose that humans can prosper and unfold their natural talents. The human mind is at once multi-talented and extremely fragile. The mind cannot begin to express itself until the conditions are conducive to personal growth. This is obvious when we look at the creativity of the Western mind compared to people caught in Asian dictatorships. The second core belief in monotheism is that individuals are required to actively achieve accomplishments. Accomplishments allow the human brain to achieve a life of value and meaning. We see this concept in the Bible's directives to observe the commandments, many of which require actions or activities.

15   While we have the BBH and Brit Milah combining to make a powerful treaty of both Zerah and Land. However, this is not the completion of the treaty. Due to a combination of factors the transfer is being delayed. These issues range from Ishmael and Hagar being expelled from his home (clearly stated) to Abimelach refusing to complete a peace treaty (inferred from the fact that Isaak needed to recut the treaty since Abimelach and Pichol left before the required meal was eaten). The result of these issues is

that Abraham is facing deep sadness. We understand that Abraham is given the test of the Binding of Isaak to reassure Abraham that his failure to convert the Canaanites was because of their idiosyncracies and not due to a lack of belief on his part.

Previously we were able to show a decline in Abraham's outlook from the BBH to the Brit Milah which indicated a serious change in mood. We did this by pointing out the two times the Bible gives us Abraham's thoughts. In modern parlance, we would describe his uncharacteristic negativity as Abraham's depression. With the other factors that are listed in the chapters after the Bris Milah, the depression must have been intense. Other factors to affect his equanimity would be his failure to ultimately save Sodom and the the sending away of Hagar and Ishmael.This pile on of failures would explain why G-d gave the "Binding of Isaak" challenge as a method to heal Abraham from depression. Providing him with a mission that he was able to succeed at G-d gave him a sense of accomplishment. We are given a hint that Abraham understood and appreciated this kindness because once Isaak is saved he could have left the mountain but instead he stays and brings his first recorded animal sacrifice to thank G-d. The display of trust and belief in G-d produced even more blessings. The blessing "and through you all the families of the world will be blessed" is the completion of the three-part treaty (Brit Bein Habasorim, Brit Melah, Binding of Isaak) between G-d and Abraham. Abraham's inducements to leave Haran are the flowchart for all the blessings bestowed at the Britot. Since the blessing of "the whole world will be blessed through your seed" (*Genesis* 12:3) was listed last on the list of the inducements, it now becomes the last of the blessings. *Genesis* 22:18(and through you all the families of the world will be blessed). This further emphasizes that there is indeed a three-part treaty and must be seen as such. Arriving at the final draft was not simple. There was a change in strategy, from the universal mission to the parochial Baini oou baincha. Also, it took many years of development, beginning with the BBH, through Isaak's birth until he was thirty-five, Ultimately, the final product will still require the Israelites to complete the treaty prior to conquering the land.

Made in the USA
Columbia, SC
03 November 2024